Homo Gaia
REJOINING EARTH'S COMMUNITY, WHERE WE BELONG

Homo Gaia

REJOINING EARTH'S COMMUNITY,
WHERE WE BELONG

Oy Kanjanavanit

First published and distributed in 2025 by
River Books Press Ltd.
396/1 Maharaj Road, Phraborommaharajawang,
Bangkok 10200 Thailand
Tel: (66) 2 225-0139, 2 225-9574
Email: order@riverbooksbk.com
www.riverbooksbk.com
@riverbooks riverbooksbk Riverbooksbk

Copyright collective work © River Books, 2025
Copyright text and images © Oy Kanjanavanit,
except where otherwise indicated.

All rights reserved. No part of this book may be reproduced or transmitted in any form or by any means, electronic or including photocopy, recording or any other information storage and retrieval system, without prior permission in writing from the publisher.

Publisher: Narisa Chakrabongse
Editor: Narisa Chakrabongse
Cover Design: Benjarat Aiemrat
Design: Ruetairat Nanta

ISBN 978 616 451 093 7

Publisher: River Books Press Ltd., Bangkok, Thailand
EU Authorised Representative: Easy Access System Europe Oü,
16879218 - Mustamäe tee 50, 10621 Tallinn, Estonia,
gpsr.requests@easproject.com

Printed and bound in Thailand by Parbpim Co., Ltd

Contents

Foreword by Belinda Stewart-Cox … 8

Prologue: Alice in Salish Wonderland … 14

Chapter 1: Feel, to be aware … 22

Chapter 2: Connect, to be whole … 30

Chapter 3: Expand our basic senses … 36

Chapter 4: Go beyond the realm of the senses … 66

Chapter 5: Access the wild wisdom … 80

Chapter 6: Communicate across species … 90

Chapter 7: Co-create together … 108

Chapter 8: Blend the outer and the inner worlds … 120

Epilogue: Towards *Homo gaia* … 132

Appendix

Daily Practice Routine … 144

From the author … 150

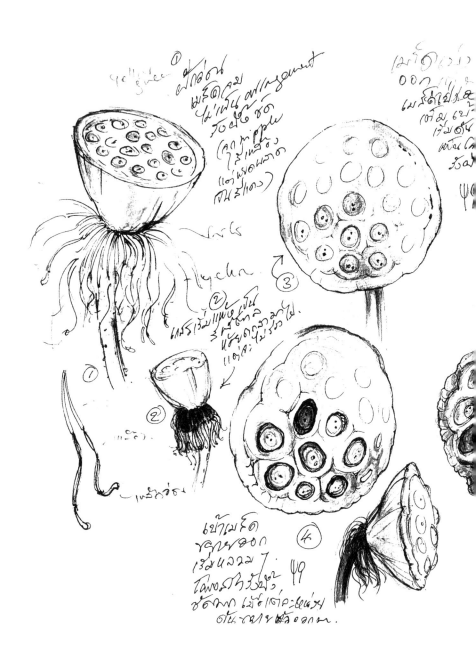

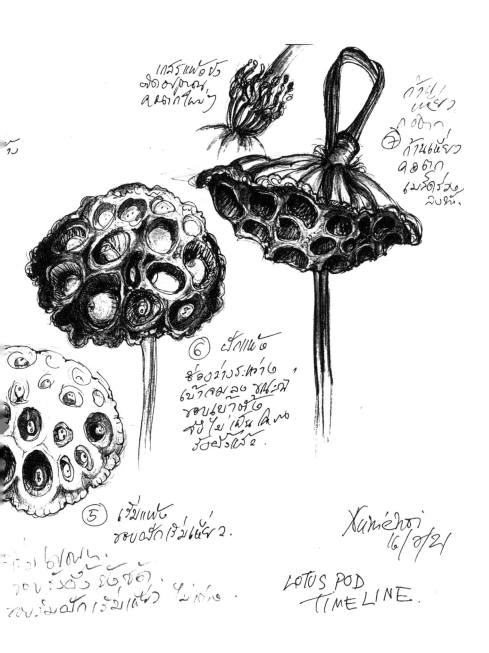

Foreword

by Belinda Stewart-Cox, OBE
British Asian Trust with Elephant Family

Have you ever felt a visceral thrill of recognition, while reading a book, when the author explains thoughts or feelings you've had but were not aware you'd had, or did not think to put them into words to make your sub-conscious conscious? That is what happened to me, repeatedly, as I read *Homo Gaia*, Oy Kanjanavanit's remarkable book of revelations.

It did not come as a surprise to me that Dr Oy has written such a clear, illuminating account of her own journey of discovery, for I have known her almost 40 years and have watched her grow from the nature-inspired PhD student doing fire ecology fieldwork in Huai Kha Khaeng, the wildlife sanctuary that was also my home-away-from-home for over a decade, to an inspiring project leader and nature-writer. From her I learned that insects can be used by citizen-science conservation programmes to assess the quality and status of a waterway – information I have shared widely – and I learned that lichens are excellent indicators of habitat health and urban pollution. So simple, so interesting, and so practical. All you need is cheap, simple equipment, pencil and paper, and a laminated guide that is relevant to your area like the one she produced for concerned students around Thailand.

The thesis at the heart of *Homo Gaia* is that most of us educated, technology-dependent, urban-influenced *Homo sapiens* have become so divorced from nature that we do not use the multiple senses we are born with and therefore do not engage fully with our environment. We often look without really seeing, hear without really listening, and think without feeling. We rarely deploy our senses of smell, touch, or taste as fully as we could to make unconscious perceptions conscious. Moreover, we regularly ignore, or disregard, the insights of our intuition, those gut feelings that are often more reliable than rational analysis because they take into account a broader spectrum of messages from our environment, both internal and external, than those we consciously consider.

Homo Gaia is enormous fun to read because Oy does not rant or preach or tell us what we should think or do. She tells stories about her own sensory discoveries, some of them quite personal, and then invites us to have a go at putting into practice what she has learned. Her tone is so engagingly conversational and encouraging that you cannot resist. You will find yourself adopting owl eyes, as I did, to register your peripheral vision, using your nose like a hound to map surrounding scents, and listening more acutely to the sounds around, many of which you hadn't heard before. Touch, taste, feel – senses that evoke memories and meanings long forgotten – and scores of other senses that we no longer think of as senses. Balance, beauty, wonder, joy. All linked to our emotional wellbeing and our ability to give or feel compassion and love.

Am I sounding a bit woo-woo? I hope not, because Oy's style is a brilliant balance of ordinary, everyday observations and experiences – all beautifully described – with the scientific data that explains them. She is that marvellous combination of scientist, traveller and artist who melds the mind of an adult with the curiosity of a child.

She opens the book by describing the transformative, almost mystical experience, she had in North America's Salish Sea when she felt unexpectedly blessed by Gaia, the Greek Goddess of Mother Earth. She then invites us to join her on a quest to find out how to access the world of inter-species communication that runs parallel to the physical world we know – a skill we all had but have forgotten how to use. With characteristic humility, she tells us that she does not know all the answers but would like us to explore the questions together because she believes it is important for the future of humanity.

Thus she sets the style and tone of *Homo Gaia*. A light-hearted but deeply serious exploration of ways we can "connect to be whole". She is motivated by her heart-felt failure to stop construction of the devastating dams across the Mekong river, the life-source of myriad species and cultures in five major biomes from the Tibetan highlands to the South China Sea. She learned then that data alone, whether facts or figures, is not persuasive. People need to feel to be properly aware, to understand the campaign slogans from within. And so, in only ten chapters, Oy takes us on a wondrous journey of learning and self-discovery. On the way she explains the science behind the phenomena we read about and, she hopes, experience. It is a work of extraordinary insight and erudition, illustrated with personal observations and anecdotes.

At one point she tells the story of her husband opting to have a tooth removed without anaesthetic because he wanted to feel the pain so fully that it numbed him. I had a similar experience, aged eight, when I gashed my foot on broken glass and needed multiple stitches. Thanks to a botched injection two years before, I was terrified of needles. I bawled so loudly that the doctor offered to stitch my foot without anaesthetic. I accepted, forgetting that stitching needs needles. "It will hurt" he said. It didn't. I felt nothing but gratitude and relief. I've not lost my fear of needles, but I have learned to control the fear and ignore the discomfort. Nowadays, I can handle stinging nettles without gloves by thinking of their stings as free acupuncture. A health bonus, in fact. It works a treat, every time.

I cannot claim any credit for this book other than the fact that I urged Oy, most emphatically, to translate her Thai original into English. To my eternal regret, I do not read Thai and therefore had no access to the book she wrote during covid lockdown. As she described it, and knowing how broadly knowledgeable she is, thematically and geographically, I knew the book was both timely and globally relevant. I wanted non-Thai speakers as well as Thai-speakers to know why she had coined the aspiration 'Homo Gaia', linking that well-known concept to our impoverished and impoverishing selves, persuading us how and why we must care more about Mother Earth, the only home we have. Most of all I wanted to read the book myself, to learn from it, and to put its insights and perspectives into practice.

I was therefore mighty chuffed, and hugely honoured, to be asked to write this foreword. I urge you all to read the book. It is fascinating, intriguing, instructive, inspiring and, most of all, it is fun. I loved it. Oy's enthusiasm, that god within (*en theo*) that motivates her, is so infectious.

Belinda Stewart-Cox, OBE

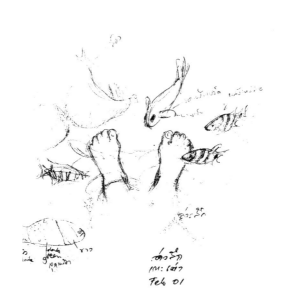

Homo Gaia

Homo
A genus of primates, which is an order of animals with opposable thumbs, giving them gripping hands with dexterity. The *Homo* is a kind of human who stand and walk on two legs. The brain is large in proportion to body size. Today there is only one species left: the *Homo sapiens* or "Wise Human". It has evolved over 200,000 years ago, multiplied in number and spread all over the world. It has created a huge impact on the environment, to such a severe level as to change the global climate.

Gaia
Gaia is the name of the ancient Greek Goddess of Mother Earth. James Lovelock, an English atmospheric scientist, used it to name his ecological theory, which sees the Earth as an animated entity, where life forms interact with each other and with inorganic components to create a complex self-regulating system that helps to maintain the conditions conducive for life on earth.

Homo gaia
A species of human that renews its membership with the Earth community, living along side other beings. It is a human that has evolved beyond the crisis of nature destruction caused by *Homo sapiens*.

Prologue
Alice in Salish Wonderland

"Forces of nature act in a mysterious manner"
~ Mahatma Gandhi

I suppose I have to start with what happened to me in 2007. It was in the late spring, not far from the Lummi Reserve, a sacred land belonging to the Lummi people, native North Americans of the Puget Sound who call themselves Lhaq'temish, meaning "People of the Sea". These sea people inhabit the coastal land of the North West Pacific, an area known as the Salish Sea. It is a land embedded with ancient spirits of Native Americans deeply connected with nature. The vista is surrounded by several majestic snow-clad volcanoes. Although much of the former pristine nature has been destroyed, there lingers a scent of certain wilderness that humans have not suppressed.

I received a grant from the Kinship Conservation Fellows that brought together 18 conservationists from many countries around the world, spending one month in the State of Washington not far from the US-Canada border, to explore how to use economic tools in nature conservation.

But what happened had absolutely nothing to do with economics. It was not even something we are familiar with in contemporary human societies.

Before the programme began, the grant management welcomed us with a special outing – a kayak trip along the coastline of Lummi Island, which was large enough to have some original forests remaining intact. The destination was a picnic at Lummi Rocks, a small rocky islet outcrop not far from the main island. The kayak tour leader was a wheelchair-bound man named Dave. Though he had lost the use of his legs, his upper body was muscled and strong. His face and eyes emitted a kind of light that commanded respect.

That morning we all helped to carry the kayaks over the forested dunes, laying them out on the beach. The tide was low, receded down to the sea grass zone, inviting me to want to run down and explore the seashore life hidden among the vegetation as I did as a kid. I picked a bit of bright green sea lettuce to taste as I absorbed the sense of place.

Before we took off, Dave asked us of our expectations for the day's outing.

Everyone was reasonable and gave polite answers along the lines of not expecting anything, just happy being out here amid such beautiful nature. Then it was my turn as the last person to respond. I don't know what came over me, perhaps it was a ripple from the open blue sky and the expansive sea, but I suddenly blurted out that I was so happy to be here, but it would be truly wonderful if we got to see an orca and a sea otter as well. After all, the sea around here was the home of orca or killer whale. Something someone from the tropical Gulf of Thailand had never seen.

My American colleagues exclaimed in unison – that's too much to ask, besides there are no sea otters around here, one needs to go down south to California[1]. As for orcas, one needs to go to the islands around San Juan or Victoria on Vancouver Island, not around here.

Only Dave kept a neutral expression, saying "It's possible. Orcas sometimes swim through here."

It was a rather chilly, but sunny day. We paddled in a group, out of the bay. The forest along the coastline was a patchy mosaic of Douglas fir stands interspersed with old growth forest. A bald eagle, with its distinctive white head, glided across the cliff face. We paddled past a headland into another bay with an old growth forest and a small, clear stream, trickling down into the sea.

As we paddled, a river otter appeared on the beach. We were all stunned, as they are harder to come across than sea otters in California.

While we let the kayak float in place as we watched the otter, a spotty harbour seal swam out from the beach, making a direct beeline for me, with no distraction or interest in anyone else. It stopped by the port flank of the kayak just beside my left knee. It was so close that if I had reached my hand out, I could have patted its head. The seal looked

---

1 Sea otters were once abundant in the Salish Sea, but they were hunted down for their skins and disappeared from the area.

at me with its clear liquid eyes for a short while before slipping down under the water and disappeared. Those pair of beady eyes penetrated deep down into my heart.

There are no words to convey exactly how I felt at that particular moment. My heart literally burst with joy. It was as if the atomic particles that once bonded tightly together to form my body broke out and dispersed into the air, the sea, the sun. There was a high voltage line connecting my heart and that of the seal. I was surprised, and embarrassed, like I was being proposed to in public. My face flushed red hot.

The look that interlocked with my eyes was clear and deep, revealing a wisdom that sparked certain knowledge that I could not yet fathom. It was full of kindness, good will, and perfect trust.

We are accustomed to wild animals fleeing from us. We are, after all, that cruel, fearful *Homo sapiens* to be wary of. But this harbour seal actually displayed an intention to approach me directly, as if to greet me outloud "Welcome".

We paddled on to Lummi Rock and spread out a picnic feast. It was a wonderful rocky islet, full of lichens and colourful hardy flowers that can withstand salty spray and poor gravelly soil. There were yellow *Sedum* or stonecrops similar to what we Thais call "yellow rock sponge" and which grow on high rocky mountains in Northern Thailand, and several species of purple *Allium* species, like the rich purple wild onion *Allium crispum* and the pale delicate rosy purple of a wild garlic. I scrambled happily over the boulders to explore the rocky meadow, not in the least suspecting that the magical show in the wonderland was far from over.

On our return trip, while paddling on the open sea with the snow-clad Olympus Range in the far background behind us, suddenly one colleague shouted out "Orca!".

We all turned to look, and there in front of us were a mother orca and her calf, swimming and half leaping in a row. The pair were at a distance far enough to feel safe and close enough to see clearly without binoculars. We floated in place watching them, until they disappeared towards the horizon.

In the end, as it turned out, I got to see both an otter and an orca just as I wished, with a seal acting as a show host, proudly presenting my request.

It was a magical experience. I felt blessed by Gaia, the Greek Mother Earth Goddess who oversees the balance within our planet community. At that moment, I felt physically tiny, but my heart opened and expanded. The feeling of joy dispersed far beyond me, merging particles to become one with all.

I didn't dare recount the supernatural nature of this experience to others for many years after it happened. I'm not quite sure why. Perhaps I feared appearing as a spiritual show off, someone who claims to have a special gift or has been god-picked to be a "chosen one".

But it really was my most precious personal experience. Many years have passed, yet I still think of it from time to time. The look from the seal's eyes is imprinted in my memory. I want to understand what exactly happened. Why did it happen? What is the meaning of this story not so unlike a fairy tale? I couldn't simply brush it off as a figment of my imagination. There were more than 20 other people who witnessed the incident.

None of the witnesses including me, however, had ever talked about it. It seems awkward for scientists to discuss this kind of thing, even though it was a real incident that occurred on a day when everyone was relaxed and cheerful.

It was as if my wish opened the secret door of the rabbit hole that Alice fell through, into a wonderland that has always been here, co-existing alongside the modern human world where we and wild animals don't know one another. It just wasn't as dramatic as Alice's experience. Here, the door simply slid open and let some twenty people slip through.

When I thought of writing about it, I messaged one of the people who witnessed it. Nejem Raheem is an economics professor in the United States. I wanted to know if there was something particularly special about that area of Native American land.

He answered right back without having to be reminded much of the incident, as if it was still fresh in his memory too, "There is, of course, something about the place. But it is also about you... and about the seals." Then he added, "Maybe it's an old thing with them."

Is this "old thing", I wonder, the same thing as the old ways recounted in fairy tales from different cultures around the world where animals could talk and carry out missions with humans? Is it possible that those fairy tales had some basis in an ancient reality, that once upon the time, it was common for humans to communicate with animals and plants. Did we all live in the same community as one single Planet Life Club then?

This incident was more than just individuals of different species communicating with one another. I did not just bump into the seal by chance, then our eyes interlocked and our hearts simply got connected. It was more than that. It was as if the physical world that we knew and could touch, had another dimension running parallel to it, which we hadn't noticed, though it may have been there all along.

How do we find the entrance again? What do we have to do to notice it, and why would we want to enter that other world.?

I don't know all the answers, but I would like us to explore these questions together.

Because I believe it is important for the future of humanity.

Harbour Seals
at Dead Man Island
low tide, Shark Reef
Lopez Island, WA.
6/10/08.

Chapter 1

Feel, to be aware

"Awareness is like the sun.
When it shines on things, they are transformed."

~ Thich Nhat Hanh

I stood my mouth agape, staring at the huge world atlas lying open on the floor.

The lines of the world's largest rivers drawn on the map popped up from the outspread pages. The wriggly line depicting the Mekong River glowed like a bendable neon sign, and stood out from the rest.

That was another moment of shining clarity for me.

It was 2003. I had taken an assignment from *Sarakadee Magazine* – a kind of Thai version of National Geographic. They wanted to do a cover theme on the Mekong River, and asked me to write an article on its ecology. There were plans to build many dams on the river and its tributaries. It had become a contentious issue as the river flows through six countries, feeding over 65 million people. Scientists in different fields were studying various aspects of the river, from the diversity of the fish species and their life cycles to the movement of river sediments. But at the time when I had to write the article, most of the research was not yet done and published.

I didn't have enough data and I didn't quite know what to do. So I thought I'd better step back to look at the big picture, while we were waiting for the details.

I took down the huge world atlas from my bookshelf, and opened the page with "Large Rivers of the World".

I had a flash of insight when I saw this picture, which is simplified here:

Suddenly, it all made sense. I understood immediately how special Mekong River was.

If ranked by length, the Mekong comes in as the world's 12th longest river, and the 18th when ranked by the volume of water discharged. Yet, when one compares the richness of fish species known to us at that time, the Mekong would rank number two worldwide, second only to the Amazon, even though there were far fewer surveys of it than major rivers in Europe and North America.

What makes the Mekong richer than so many rivers that are greater in length and size?

An answer screamed out from the world map. The reasons were laid out on the pages in front of me.

The Mekong is one of the few great rivers that flows down a longitude line. It passes many biomes from the snowy roof top of the world on the Tibetan High Plateau, through the temperate zone and sub-tropics of China, to the seasonal monsoonal climate of mainland Southeast Asia, all the way down to the nearly equatorial tropic of the delta in South Vietnam.

The Nile, of course, also flows along a longitude line, but it passes through desert and semi-desert, before it ends in a dry land.

It becomes even more fascinating when the story of its geographical past is considered. Take the Ice Age for instance, when the Mekong river system was likely connected to the Sunda River that is now submerged under the Gulf of Thailand. The fishes of the two great rivers could travel between them. The more I contemplated the map, the more I became aware of how unique and special the Mekong River was. Then when an array of new research came out, it became ever more apparent that here is an ecological system so mighty, so integrated, that it is too complex for humans to master and control. We need to embrace its greatness wholeheartedly and respect it. Any development scheme we think of must complement the lives and rhythms of the river. When we embrace the natural forces that shape and drive it, the river will take care of us.

I understand totally that the map of world rivers does not mean much to the general public. My awareness of the Mekong came from my accumulated experience. It came from years of noticing and immersing myself in nature, both on land and in the water. Although my experiences were from other places, not so much from the Mekong directly, it was a knowledge that had become embedded in my body, combined with scientific information that I had accumulated. So, when I saw the map, I had a sudden insight that seemed like an instinct, although it was just a view through the lens of science.

For those without similar experiences, this image is likely to mean not much more than just another map. To make the Mekong meaningful to others, we knew we would need to communicate in a way that was relatable. We could try to touch people with breathtaking images of its magnificent scenery; make people exclaim in amazement when extraordinary stories of the river were told, about the wonderful wildlife and their life cycles, about the relationship between people and the river, about the ways of the river and the diverse ways all the kinds of life that depend on the river adapt to it.

At the policy level, we had to interpretate its intrinsic values in monetary terms, showing its economic importance from the level of basic livelihood survival to national GDP. To investors, we needed to point out the risks that came with a project that stood to create negative impacts on so many peoples' lives and had the potential of escalating into international conflicts – something that is hardly good for business.

Many people from all kinds of disciplines who cared about the life of the Mekong contributed their expertise and all helped to explain the utmost importance of looking after the river together. They all tried to show the immense negative impacts on so many dimensions from constructing dams across the main channel of this great river, in particular the Xayaburi Dam in Laos, built by a Thai company, which was going to obstruct the migratory passage used by fish to reach the pebble river bed upstream where they lay their eggs.

It was an immense effort, but we all failed. We couldn't even get the mainstream public interested, let alone stop the destruction. The Mekong remained a distant issue, far removed from Bangkok, from the city where people voices are heard.

We tried talking money, but it was hardly meaningful when the money in question related to the economy of other countries that depended on resources from the Mekong, money that supported the lives of more than 60 million people that was about to dwindle and disappear, rather than the cash flow in and out of the bank accounts of powerful decision makers.

I need to emphasise at this point that Thailand did not need more power supply. Usually a power reserve of 15% is deemed sufficient, but Thailand had more than a 50% reserve. This is pure available energy supply. It is what we have even before considering other alternative power sources and numerous measures in power management that would help to reduce electricity demand. There was absolutely no need whatsoever to kill the Mekong for electricity supply from the Xayaburi Dam.

The Mekong River today is like a very sick mother, in a comatose state. Not only are 100s of fish species unable to their loads of eggs to lay on the oxygenated riverbed above the dam, but a huge amount of sediments – more than half of the entire river sediment load – are held back behind the dams instead of being washed downstream. These sediments are natural fertilizers that farmers along the Mekong and around the connecting great lake Tonle Sap of Cambodia are waiting for. Usually as the river flood retreats, the sediment is left coating the ground, ready for rice seeds to be sown. The worst impact is at the delta in South Vietnam. When there is not enough sediment being washed down and settling downstream to build up the land, the sea invades and erodes it, to the extent that Vietnam is losing land at more than 5 metres per year.

The pattern of water flow is no longer seasonal. The amount and timing of water discharges now correlate with dam operations. It no longer matches with the cycles of life downstream. So, for instance, in the dry season when river islets and beaches emerge above the river channel, and it's the time when many birds lay eggs on those temporary sandy outcrops, the dams upstream would release huge volumes of water that flood the islets and birds' nests.

All the information was converted into numbers to present to the decision makers in Thailand, including those banks that decided to give loans for the construction of the Xayaburi Dam. After some consideration, one big banker brushed me off casually, saying all the so-called scientific information that the world-class experts had studied was merely an opinion of one group of people, they were not facts.

I wouldn't have minded at all if he had said that because I showed him my Wonder Rivers of the World map that only I found exciting. But to so casually dismiss all the data and its implications?

This issue is not much different from the crisis of climate change.

We have enough solid scientific data, but a lot of humans remain unperturbed.

Clearly, scientific information alone is not enough to change people's minds.

We need new systems and new rules to facilitate our co-existence on this planet. These things can only happen through political drive at many levels, born out of collective consciousness among a group of people large enough to spark a flame in a society. The collective consciousness of individuals – that one, this one, those two, those three, and so on.

If we look back at humanity's history of change it often starts modestly. England's abolition of the slave trade in 1807, for example, began with a few Quaker housewives some 100 years before, until with continuous efforts it grew into a movement.

A new collective consciousness always begins with a few individuals.

But what is it that created awareness in those individuals' hearts in the first place?

By awareness, I do not mean having received information.

The word 'awareness' in Thai is used widely, but it has become so flippant, so over-used that it is now one of the most meaningless words in the Thai vocabulary. We Thais are so accustomed to a culture of creating slogans to generate 'awareness' that we are bored stiff of the word, and are ready to dismiss it. Kids of my generation had an earful and an eyeful of government slogans on streetside billboards, from "Work is Money, Money is Work, Creating Happiness" during the 1960s under the regimes of Field Marshal Sarit Thanarat and subsequently Field Marshal Thanom Kittikachorn, through the "Love the King, Care About Your Children, Help Resist Addictive Drugs" of the 1980s and 1990s, to the recent "Forests confer Benefit, Support Our Lives", "Stop Global Warming With Sufficiency Economy" and "Grow Up Not Corrupt" of this past decade.

Clearly slogans on billboards alone do not solve problems. We do what we are told not to do all the time.

In meetings on the crisis of the heating planet and collapsing ecological system, organizers typically invite a man of powerful status to give a keynote speech inaugurating the event. He will invariably complain about the lack of awareness among the general public. Meanwhile the meetings themselves tend to create a huge amount of unnecessary waste, from plastic water bottles to cotton tote bags, perhaps the 100th free bag each of us has received from such events over the past few years.

The word 'awareness' in Thai is thus shallow and superficial. Give out the information, a brief FYI, and the job is done. Let's change the topic.

But something that I witnessed in the early 2010s made me change my thoughts on the meaning of the word. We were campaigning for bicycle-friendly cities at the time. We argued that cycling is an important component of a city that is friendly to life – a city that is a human habitat.

It was blistering hot that afternoon. I don't remember exactly what we were doing or where we were going, but I ended up cycling through the Bangkok streets with a bunch of young people in their twenties. We went along the shade-less, sun-baked, 10-lane Sathorn Road, where the concrete reflected solar heat with no mercy. Then we crossed the junction and rode into the tree-clad Wireless Road, which was just as wide as Sathorn Road, but all the lanes were well shaded with huge raintrees. Their big branches stretched out far and wide creating a tree canopy over the entire road surface; some of the trees were aged around a hundred years or more.

The temperature on our skin dropped suddenly by 5 degree Celcius. If we were sitting in an air-conditioned car with tinted windows, the only thing we would probably feel as we slid into Wireless Road is the beauty of the greenery, relaxing and pleasing to the eyes. But cyclists feel everything on the road – the sights, sounds, smells, dust, wind, heat and coolness. We receive information with our entire bodies.

Many of my young companion riders that day have since turned to campaigning for city big trees.

We have all known about the benefits of trees since we were little. At primary school we were taught about plant photosynthesis. We know trees not only give oxygen but clean up the air we breathe. They give us cool shade. They are good beings, offering many benefits, blah, blah, blah…

This is information we received with the grey lump on the left side of our brains. We all know it. We were all taught it. But through living in a densely built city, we live in sealed homes, sealed schools and offices, and sealed malls. It's not often we get to truly feel the value of trees through direct experience that imprints the knowing in our bodies.

Knowing with our heads, when big trees are cut down, we may think what a shame. But knowing with our entire body, the pain is felt in our hearts as we understand how our lives are intricately linked with the trees. We do not just receive information, but it is imprinted into our bodies and minds.

The word 'awareness' in Thai is *tra-nak-roo*, meaning 'imprinted knowing'. It is a wisdom from our bodies that stay with us for a long time.

When the information one received a long time ago becomes a personal experience, coolness from tree shade is no longer just a thought, but a personal truth.

One of my sister-in-laws turned vegetarian when she saw a pick-up truck, carrying caged pigs to slaughter, drove past a roadside restaurant where she was enjoying a plate of slow-cooked pork leg stew. She had of course seen pig trucks many times before, and she was well-informed on the life of industrial pigs going to slaughter houses, but something in the pigs' eyes looking at her from the tight, hot cage, with no room to move, went straight to her heart. It hit her so hard, that it made her change her diet.

In that very second, she and the pigs, and other animal friends of the pigs, became related like brothers and sisters.

What about you? Have you had this kind of experience, when a true awareness of something is born within you.

The moment when known information becomes awareness.

What happened?

How did it happen?

Chapter 2

Connect, to be whole

> "Forget not that the earth delights to feel your bare feet and the winds long to play with your hair."
>
> ~ Khalil Gibran

I grew up in an era before towns were lit up brightly at night, hazing the sky with artificial light pollution that blocks out most starlight from our sight. Lying on a balcony by the sea looking at the night sky full of stars was hardly an unusual event. I was a generation that grew up with stars.

Even so, while there were regular nights full of stars, there were also ultra-star-studded nights. One starriest starry night is still imprinted in my memory. I was a teenager, just graduated from high school. It was my gap year and I took a volunteer job at Doi Angkhang Royal Highland Agricultural Project in Northern Thailand. At the time it was very remote and a rather difficult place to get to. We had a diesel electricity generator in the central building for just a few hours in the evening. Some nights the system would fail for whatever reason, and we would light candles and lamps instead.

In the highlands above 1,000 metres, the atmosphere tends to be clearer than in the lowlands. I felt since my first night there, that the stars were really beautiful. Then, one night, things just shot up to another level. The sky was crystal clear. There were no clouds and no moonlight. Nothing came in between me and all the stars in the entire universe. It was just an empty space. I could see clouds of star dusts and the milky way bridge stretched across the sky over my head.

I remember it so vividly. I understood what it was to feel as one with everything. At that moment everything was complete. Nothing was missing. I did not need or want anything else anymore.

I is interesting that when I ask people to tell me of a moment they felt joy with nature or simply at peace and happy with their surroundings, many would speak of a magical night full of glimmering stars.

I am not quite sure why starry skies have such an impact upon us.

Perhaps it reminds us unconsciously of our origin, from the birth of universe, and the ultimate source of our being. Details of our daily life that seemed so important an hour ago become insignificant.

That kind of pure joy can also occur in other moments with nature. It could be an early morning in a rice field, where the fog has left sparkling dew droplets like little diamonds on spider webs, making them seem like delicate gem-studded lacey shawls belonging to the fairies.

Or it could be a sad, lonely day, when a little bird flew down to perch on the bench next to you, and suddenly everything was better.

I'd like to invite you to revisit your feelings at those one-with-nature moments in detail, both the feeling in your heart and the sensation in your body.

Many say that in that moment they feel tiny. They are nothing important and grand. Yet they're full of incredible joy, as awareness expands far and wide, becoming one with everything. They feel open and light. It's a moment of completion.

These accounts are just as the Indian yogi Sadhguru said. He explains that it is human nature to yearn to expand. We have this drive as a foundation. When our basic survival needs are met, we don't want to limit ourselves within that boundary. We want more. We want to expand. But our expansion tends to take on a dimension that can never be fulfilled. We grapple for material things and worldly goods. We want to be richer, we want more power, we want more fame, we want more acceptance – want, want, want, ever more wanting.

But in the state when our awareness expands to intermesh with all others as one, we know we are complete. We are far more than our physical body. We've found our nature, which is as big as the universe.

In such a moment, we are aware that we are part of the most incredible, most wonderful, most magical network there ever was. Its inter-connection is more complex and profound that any ecological textbook could attempt to explain. Everything is new and fresh as if we are seeing them for the first time.

Of course, that state of being does not last in ordinary, unenlightened humans like you and I. The act of remembering, however, pulls up a faint scent of that state to remind us of our vast connection to all beings.

I like to hear people telling their own stories of personal connecting experiences. When the box of receptivity opens, the light in their eyes changes and a glimmer of joy appears.

The New Age movement noted that in an extremely relaxed state our brain waves correlate with the "Earth's Heartbeat" or the electromagnetic frequencies of 7.83 hertz in the planet's lower ionosphere, created from thunderstorms and lightning. It was first predicted by Winfried Otto Schumann, so is sometimes called the "Schumann Resonance" in honour of the physicist.

Generally, when we are in our working mode, in other words engaged in a task that requires thinking, our brain waves are at the frequency range of 13-35 hertz. This is the beta wave. In a more alert beat-the-deadline state, the frequencies are faster, somewhat in the middle of the range. If we are stressed or angry, it goes fast into high beta. In a contemplative mode when we are considering something of interest, it goes slower in low beta waves.

Slower still in a relaxed and calm, no thinking state, brain wave frequencies are in alpha wave, ranging between 8-12 hertz.

In a meditative state, we are in the band of theta wave, 4-7 hertz.

And in deep sleep, the brain slows down to delta wave at 0.5-4 hertz.

The earth's heartbeat frequency of 7.8 hertz falls right in between alpha and theta.

That is why natural therapists make their clients slow down, relax, and feel sleepy. They try to get their brains out of thinking mode. In this deeply relaxed state, our nervous systems and various parts of the brain start to synchronize and tune in with the frequencies of natural beings, in the rhythm of the earth's heartbeat.

However, I don't think we need to sit down to meditate or make ourselves ultra-slow to keep the brain in alpha wave. Relaxed brain waves can exist in the waking state while performing activities.

From my personal experience and from exchanges with different poeple, many moments when we felt perfect joyous peace of being one with nature, we were not drowsy. We were not physically slow.

In fact, all too often, slowness comes with numbness. We sometimes mistake that numb state with being calm and at peace, whereas it is likely to be more akin to anaesthesia – a senseless state when we do not receive information from the world around us.

The numbness includes being apathetic to all the wonderful phenomena we witness every day. Become more aware – all the things around us, and all the things inside us, are such incredible wonders. We and other living beings are real magicians performing alchemy. The plants with their green leaves do that ingenious act called photosynthesis, converting intangible energy from the sun into chemical energy that we can grasp, eat, and accumulate. Yet, we do not turn into plants. Instead, they are converted into our physical body through our digestive system and memories within our cells and DNA. While photosynthesizing, plants give off oxygen, which we breathe in and which burns fuel from food to sustain our lives. Everything coordinates with one another in perfect unison, full of intelligence. We really should wake up and be fascinated with it every day. Instead, we are numb and indifferent to all these most magical realities.

The state of knowing we are one with nature is the opposite of numbness. It is joy suffused with a light vibration. This is when the total body is awake, not blissfully numb. It is not the same as being alert, watching out for dangers, but is a state of being fully awake in stillness. We know what is going on, and delight in the wonders around us.

It is a state when the boundary between us and other living things begins to dissolve.

More important than a slow speed is perhaps the process of perceiving the world around us.

It begins with the senses that we have.

Pittosporum sp.
Daintree – Cape Tribulation N.P.
May 98.

Chapter 3
Expand our basic senses

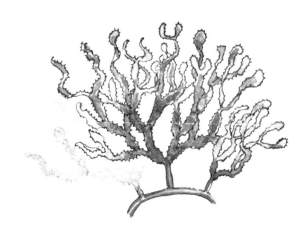

> "The world is full of magical things, patiently waiting for our senses to grow sharper."
>
> ~ William Butler Yeats

I once talked to my mother about our earliest memories. The time I could remember well with details of scenes and even conversations was when I was three years old, the age I started to walk to a kindergarten near our home. Yet, I vaguely recalled another feeling of being in my mother's arms and her lifting me up to smell some white frangipani flowers.

My mother was very surprised by this because she actually had done that when I was a newborn baby at Bangkok Nursing Home, where there was a row of white frangipani trees growing along the garden, before the hospital was renovated and expanded. Another time I stayed at that hospital was when I got stung by a carpenter bee and almost died at eight months old. My mother stayed the night with me and carried me outside when I recovered to smell the frangipani flowers as she did when I was born.

The memory may have come from that time when I was eight months old, but that is still a pre-toddler age, which makes it all the more surprising.

The things I remember are a combination of feelings and senses: the scent of the flowers, my mother's arms, and the sight of that sprig of white frangipani.

I should emphasize here that being able to recall such an early memory has nothing to do being brainy. I was never a genius. I was just a normal, rather bright kid. Nothing extraordinary.

But that sensory experience imprinted deeply.

Senses are tools we living beings use to receive information about what is going on in the world around us. When a single-celled organism appeared on this planet 3,500 million years ago, it was just a bag that could multiply itself, but there was an inside and an outside of its body.

It could detect and respond to changes in the environment through the thin membrane, making it different from inanimate objects.

Early senses in the evolution of life concern the reception of information in the immediate vicinity, be it detecting the surrounding chemicals, or tactile sensing the movement of water currents or pressure on the body. It's an aid to survival, whether to stay put in that same place of abundance or whether there is a reason to find a new niche.

As life and habitats evolved into more complex systems, living beings needed more information to survive. An ability to receive information at a remote distance became an advantage. It is useful to be able to detect necessary resources which are further away and it is helpful if one can sense and avoid danger before coming face to face with it.

Our bodies and sensory systems have co-evolved on this planet together with the other life forms we have interacted with. Not only have we been using our senses to hide from predators, search for food, and propagate, but the bodies that we see as our own are also composed of many species of living organisms.

The line of research that has shaken the field of health care in a big way in this 21st century is the discovery that only half of our body is made up of our own cells; the other half or sometimes more than half consists of all kinds of microbes living and going about their business in their habitat, which is our body. These microbes worked together to enhance efficiency of various processes that sustain our life.

Our body is therefore a walking ecosystem that needs to interact with other ecosystems, just like the sea exchanges minerals with rivers at the deltas. We need to take beneficial microbes into our bodies, through the food that we eat, the air that we breathe, and the things we touch, in order to maintain our immune system, digestive system, and even the release of hormones. It has been found that healthy people contain a high diversity of microbes comparable to the richness of species in a tropical rainforest, while in less healthy people the microbe community low in diversity may be likened to a desert.

Our human body has been evolving this way for a long time. If we count from the time when our path split off from our common ancestor with the chimpanzees, it would be around seven million years ago. If we prefer to focus on *Homo sapiens* evolution, then that has been over 200,000 years.

Hardly surprising then that both our physical and mental health are depended on our close relationship with nature.

Suddenly, however, in just the past few decades, the human way of life has changed drastically with technology that has created a totally new culture disconnected from nature. We spend most our time in air-conditioned buildings, wearing shoes and walking on smooth flat floors, staring at computer screens for most part of the day.

The senses that we mainly use are our eyesight, focusing on a narrow frame in the immediate distance in front of us, while our ears hear loud noises. We are constantly subjected to over-powering stimulants, to the extent that we start to believe that our bodies, ears, eyes, noses, tongues are limited to sensing within these narrow bands of receptivity.

But our body is not that much different from that of our ancestors, who used to be able to detect the presence of a Sabre-toothed tiger waiting behind a boulder to ambush a human baby on its mother's back. It is also the same kind of body that used to find water in the middle of a desert; the body that needed to use all its senses to gather detailed information from its surroundings if it was to survive. These capabilities had to be developed through interactions with other species. Now that body cannot adjust to new changes at the same rate as the rapid advancement of technology and culture.

The irony is while we have grown accustomed to the comforts of a modern insulated, indoor lifestyle, it does not actually correspond with the real needs of our body. This is particularly crucial for children who cannot develop fully without interacting with nature. Many symptoms often appear, collectively known as "Nature Deficit Disorder", a term coined by Richard Louv in his 2005 landmark book *Last Child in the Woods*, such as Attention Deficit Disorder (ADD), mood swings and extreme tantrums, poor balance, poor coordination of limbs, body parts and movements.

But these capabilities can be recovered. They're still within us. They're just dormant.

How many senses do we have? Experts have yet to agree on the actual number, but there are certainly many more than the basic five that Aristotle identified – sight, hearing, smell, taste, and touch. Just on the category of tactile alone, there are far more than simple contact on the skin. We often take them for granted until those capabilities are compromised. Take sense of balance for example. Normally we hardly think of it, and only recognize its vital importance when we get vertigo.

There are currently a number of sensory groupings. Some author identifies 7 senses, some 9, some 12, and others recognize 18, 21,24, 32, even as many as 53 senses. It partly depends on the objective of each particular author.

In the process of perceiving the world around us, we start with the sensory system detecting what's happening, then sending signals to memory units to interpret them with information that we have been accumulated throughout our lives. For humans and other vertebrates, the brain is the main organ that does the job, leading to our responses to whatever is happening. Whether it is an unintentional automatic response or a deliberate decision to respond, depends on our cultivated habit in a given situation. Buddhist practice emphasizes observing this sensing process as a foundation for cultivating mindfulness, so we develop an ability to choose our responses instead of merely reacting to whatever triggers us. It is often said to be an empowerment, when *respond* is combined with *ability* it becomes *responsibility* for our own actions.

It is a fascinating process with many steps if we look at the working of neurons or nerve cells in detail. It starts with a sensory organ getting stimulated, which then sends information in the form of chemical molecules and electrical signals, from cell to cell to cell, all the way to the brain. The information received is sent to a corresponding part of the brain to interpret and command various reactions. This includes the releasing of chemicals that impact our emotions, depending on the brain's interpretation.

This multi-step process appears to happen in a split second, but if we can observe and monitor it in time, we can train our sensory system to be an incredibly effective and powerful information-receiving tool.

The modern lifestyle with its over-powering stimulants has dulled our senses. We need to retrain them, sharpen them to detect finer information, by slowing down and observing every moment better. We can then explore the capacity of our senses, see how much more they can expand, how much wider and further, becoming more detailed and more subtle.

We can then contemplate the information we receive and see what happens to us.

This book divides the core senses into categories that are relevant in the context of basic nature connection, drawing in part on the work of Jon Young of the 8 Shields Institute, who has developed many practical exercises. Jon also sees a relationship between the development of each sensory organ and the development of a corresponding attribute in our being.

SEEING
Associated Attribute: Beauty and Happiness

I start with our eyes because we are an animal species who rely most heavily on sight. As much as 80% of the information we sense is from what we see. Both our eyes are set in front like other primates, enabling us to focus on an object and assess its distance well. However, as well as having good telescopic eyesight, we also have a wide-angle lens, which we hardly ever use in screen-staring lives.

Putting on owl eyes

Find your own wide-angle lens. Stand with your spine straight, and fix your eyes on a far object in front of you. Keep your head still and focus on this point throughout the whole exercise. Stretch your arms out in front of you at eye level and wriggle your fingers. Keep wriggling your fingers while slowly spreading your arms wider and wider to the point where you cannot see your wriggling fingers from the corners of your eyes any more. Then bring the out-stretched arms in a bit until you notice the wriggling fingers at the periphery of your field of vision while your eyes still focus at the fixed object in front. This is the edge of your wide-angle lens.

Try doing the same thing with the vertical axis, until you find the uppermost and lowermost points of your peripheral vision.

This exercise is called "owl eyes" because owls have eyes set in the front of their faces like us, but they also see at a very wide angle – and so shall we. We are going to activate the owl potential of our vision.

Once you find the wide angle of your owl eyes, try walking and seeing with them. Just walk normally with your eyes looking ahead, but also be aware of things that appear in your peripheral vision. If you forget where that angle at the corners of your eyes is, simply stretch out your arms and wriggle your fingers to locate it. If you are tensed up, just blink and move your head and neck about to unwind and try again. If you keep practicing, you will find it slowly feels more natural. Try walking with owl eyes 30 minutes a day for a week, and note the difference. Are there any changes in your vision?

The things we see from the corners of our eyes tend to be some kind of movements. As we detect the movement, we then turn to focus on it. In this way, we receive more information than simply relying only on narrow telescopic vision only.

Try imagine you are an owl, perching on a branch and look out at the world around you. How is it different from seeing the world as a human?

Searching for images

Even when we look at the world with a narrow field of vision, the images we see still contain an overwhelming amount of information, which we cannot take in all at once. This is particularly true in a natural habitat. We need to train our eyes and brain to identify and filter information. But we can also practice focusing on one challenge at a time.

It is already in our nature to select and filter information. Let's start with closing your eyes and thinking of a colour – say red. Then open your eyes, the first things that catch your eyes will be red objects. Try again, close your eyes and think of the colour yellow. Open your eyes, and yellowish objects immediately kick in.

Now, try a finer challenge. Look around you, see how many shades of green you can find. The more you look, the more subtle shades of green you see. There are not only dark greens and light greens, but greens with varying amounts of blue, yellow-tinted green and greyish green.

When I was an archaeological student in England, we had to record the colours of the soil layers we excavated. There were many shades of white in the chalky soil. It became a fun challenge to describe the soil colour as accurately as possible. Our report would specify that this was a magnolia white, which is different from daisy white, and here in this layer is a latte white. Graphic artists would probably be even more specific and give the proportional percentages of CMYK.

From looking for colour, let's change to looking for shapes and various textures – shiny things or rough-skinned things, for instance. In fact try whatever challenge you can think of.

Learn to look at groups of living things you are interested in. It could be flowers, birds, insects, or whatever. When we become familiar with something, our eyes readily spot them. I remember the time when I was training my team to identify lichens, which are tiny organisms made up of fungi and algae that come and live together, growing on rocks and tree trunks. After a few weeks, everyone in the team could not not-see lichens. Even when relaxing at home watching a soap opera on TV, they automatically noticed lichens on trees in the background of a dramatic scene depicting a fight between the heroine and her evil rival. They could deduce that the air quality at the filming location was good, because the lichen species they saw on TV were the types that do not tolerate pollution well!

The inner quality that we develop when we practice seeing in this way is the ability to see beauty in all kinds of natural elements. A beautiful landscape need not be a spectacular vista of a dramatic landform at sunset. It could be a small grassy swamp that at first glance doesn't seem so pretty, yet we can see its beauty. And beauty makes us happy.

The Native American Navajo tribe has a song to celebrate the beauty surrounding us. Singing it outdoors opens the heart to be aware of the beauty of all living things, bringing their physical body in tune with their feelings. This is the English translation of the song:

Now I walk in beauty,
Beauty is before me,
Beauty is behind me,
Above and below me.

Google the tune on Youtube, and try singing it while walking in a forest or a garden.

HEARING
Associated Attribute: Quiet Mind

Have you ever wondered why we don't have an ear lid to shut out sounds although we have eye lid to shut off images?

Sounds warn us of dangers before they reach us. Sudden loud noises make us jump. Our heart beats faster, our blood pressure rises. Cortisol, the stress hormone, is released instantly to stimulate an alert response, ready to avert danger.

On the other hand, the sound of birdsong and their idle chatter relaxes us. It has long been embedded in our DNA to signify safety and normalcy.

Danger can come at any time, and we are particularly vulnerable when we're asleep, so we cannot shut off our hearing.

From the cave dwellers' fundamental need for survival, human society has developed an incredibly diverse array of ambient sounds – music, engines, and all sorts of noisy activities. The volume of sound is taken up to a new level with amplifier technology. We are now constantly surrounded by a clamouring racket.

Sounds are no longer mere warning signals. They themselves have become a danger.

It is not only sounds over 120 decibels that endanger our hearing, but sounds not quite as loud can also be detrimental to both our physical and mental health. Various noises impact the working of our body in different ways. When sound waves travel through the air and hit the liquid in our ears, they send the waves onto tiny nerve hairs that stimulate chemicals, which then transform into different electrical frequencies to reach the brain. If we are not mindful, the brain will command reactions automatically in response to the signals received. If it is a sound we dislike, the response will be irritation, stress, heart diseases, insomnia, or simply an inability to rest.

Hearing sounds is therefore a sensory system that is most associated with our peace of mind. That's why it's so important to find a quiet spot to listen to the sounds of nature every day.

Noticing Sounds
Find a shady spot in a garden where you can sit with your eyes closed, and listen to the sounds surrounding you from all directions: in front, from behind, on the left, on the right, above, and even below, as sometimes there is a sound from the ground. Note the dominant sounds. What do you readily hear? List them down. You might want to try to split them into two categories – man-made sounds and sounds from nature. The latter can be divided into subsets of animal sounds and other natural sounds like those of the wind, the water, or rustling leaves. Listen more carefully and note the finer differences. How many bird sounds are there? Expand the radius of your receptivity. Stretch your hearing further. What is the furthest quietest sound you can hear?

Notice too your own emotions. Record on your list of sounds, those you like and dislike.

Listen a little while longer. Simply observe your feeling towards the sounds you don't like. Do your feelings change at all? Check your emotions again.

Sitting still and noticing ambient sounds in detail is one of my favourite exercises whenever I feel disturbed and restless. It calms and centres me in just a few breaths. The noises that I dislike quickly become just sounds that I receive. At the same time, I become aware of all sorts of activities happening around me. It changes me from being an impacted person to an observer who is receiving information, or at least it changes me from being in a messy, over-reactive state to the still, mindful state of an observer.

Making a Sound Map

Listening to sounds provides an unending source of knowledge. Sound mapping is a classic exercise that we use to study nature through listening. As with the previous exercise, we sit still and listen to the sounds around us in all directions, but this time we also note the locations of the sources of the sounds in relation to where we are sitting in that landscape. Geographers like to use North as a reference point, so face north, and mark your location in the middle of a blank sheet of paper with an arrow pointing to the North at the edge. Listen to the sounds you hear and mark them on the paper at the directions and relative distances from where you are sitting. The marks could be words or symbolic icons representing the sounds. Loud noises could be drawn in big bold letters, for instance, while quiet sounds could be shown in light tiny lines.

Contemplate the sound map you have created. It will tell you a lot about what was going on at that place at that time, and who was doing what and where.

We can make repeated sound maps of a given place and it is particularly interesting when we combine the information from many people who were sitting at different spots. What we then get is a sound map of the habitat of our locality. It becomes a kind of treasure guide.

Noticing the directions of sounds while on a hike also helps us stay orientated to where we are. I like to note the sound of running stream in a forest as it's a useful reference point.

Listening to bird language

The next exercise is to learn to listen to birds. This is not only to identify different species of birds, but to actually understand their language. Try focusing on just one common bird species. In Thailand the garden bird the Oriental Magpie Robin is a good choice. Note the array of sounds this songbird actually makes, and observe its behaviour and activities along with those sounds. Before long, you will begin to be able to decode their language, at least to a certain extent.

Why birds?

Within the animal community, birds are like the inter-species lookouts. When there is danger looming, they give a warning call. If we learn to listen, we can more or less work out the kind of danger they are calling out. This may vary in different localities. Around my house in Bangkok, the warning call I hear every day is a fairly subdued alert they give among themselves, saying "Cat alert! Behind that car! Be careful!". The warning call rises up many levels, however, when the danger becomes a snake. Often, many bird species join forces, screeching for help from other animals, like from that human tapping away on her laptop nearby, because the snake is trying to eat their nestlings.

Greater Flameback Woodpeckers + Greater Racket-Tailed Drongos. NAC neighbourhood Kalady, Kerala 11/7/06

Chapter 3 – Expand our basic senses   47

A zoologist in South America has lived to tell tales of how he survived twice because he listened to bird alarm calls. Once it was a lurking poisonous snake on his path, the other time it was a wild cat hiding in order ambush him.

So learn to listen to the birds. There are a lot more details to learn in their language.

SMELLING
Associated Attribute: Memories & a Sense of Place

One of the most primeval senses is the ability to detect scents. It evolved long before sight and hearing. Even bacteria have this ability. It is a sense that helps us receive information about the chemical world around us at a distance a little removed from bodily contact. It is one of the first senses a baby learns to use; just as I remembered the scent of the frangipani flowers from when I was a baby.

The scents we smell are molecules that are dispersed and suspended in the air (or water for aquatic beings). When a molecule floats into our nose, all the way to the cavity at the back, it sticks to the lining fluid and dissolves into it. The area contains scent-receptor cells, and these send information directly to the part of the brain that interprets it. This is a more direct pathway than sight and sound information, which are first sent to information distribution centres in the brain to differentiate and sort out before being sent to the different parts of the brain that interpret the information. Our reactions to smells are therefore extremely fast. We back away all too fast when hit with a 'bad' odour, while immediately being drawn in a 'pleasant' fragrance.

An adult human has as many as 40 million scent-receptor cells with each having the ability to receive different scent molecules. They combine to identify a given scent, allowing us to be able to differentiate around 10,000 different smells.

Yet, often we can't quite articulate a sense of smell without referring to something else.

Is it possibly because smell is an ancient sense working directly with our primeval brain (what we often like to call the "reptilian brain"), that humans across all cultures have a relatively limited vocabulary to express smells – words like scented, stinky, smelly – just a few. It's not much richer in the Thai language either. Generally, when we describe smells, we link them with common experiences such as things or feelings, for example, pandan leaf scent, or a spicy smell.

It is also interesting that sometimes when we have a vague feel about something which we cannot pinpoint succinctly we say it has the "smell of…" something. One such example being "it smells a bit fishy to me'.

Smell reveals a hint of what has been accumulated. We ourselves have a smell of the food we eat. Likewise, plant smells can vary in different localities, even from the same species. They reflect the accumulated parts of the landscape – the minerals in the soil, sun, and water of a particular place.

Smells, therefore, work closely with memories. Its attribute is a sense of place, connecting us in time and space with different localities.

In the book *Songkram Lok Nai Singkhong* (World War in Things) by Monsicha Roongchawalnont, the Thai author recounts how Ernest Beaux, creator of the all-time favourite perfume Chanel No. 5, "blended this scent using memories from the time he was a soldier stationed at Murmansk in Russia. …Beaux was impressed with the natural beauty there, especially the refreshing scent at the edge of the lake in spring. He applied this feeling to the scent of the famous perfume. To this day, the people of Murmansk still joke around that if one fills up a bottle with the lake water, it would be like taking a bottle of Chanel No.5 home."

Since our nasal chamber and mouth are connected, smell is very closely linked with taste. The molecules from the food we eat float up to the scent-receptor zone at the back of the nasal cavity. The two senses work together to create memories of our experiences in different places. It builds up the identity of a locality.

A close friend took her aging father who was losing his memories and the will to live to lunch near the Bangpakong river delta for a change of surroundings. He had been a pioneering botanist who once spent years researching the mangroves around there. It was an hour's drive from their home, and he was quiet throughout the journey until, as they approached the delta, he began to take an interest in the passing scenery. When they reached the restaurant, there was a breeze blowing through the restaurant and the look in his eyes suddenly changed. There was a spark. He perked up and told his daughter, "Salty smell!". He remembered where he was, and he was all smiles and happy throughout the day.

Sniffing with a dog's nose
We can improve our sense of smell and our ability to discern different scents. The easiest trick is to wet your nostrils. Airborne molecules will be able to dissolve into the wall of your nasal cavity more readily, enabling you to detect scents more clearly right away. Note that the noses of healthy dogs – the sniffing champions – they are always wet.

Once you begin to notice more, record your observations.

Try to sniff an object closely. Take a hard, short sniff – ftt-ftt. Think about the scent you detect and try to explain it. You may connect it to something you know, an experience, a feeling, a sound that stirs up an emotion. There is no right or wrong way to describe things. It is your personal experience, your memory.

Pair up with a friend, and get them to hand you different things to smell while you close your eyes (non-toxic things please!). Guess the objects that you smell.

Walk about and sniff things throughout the house. What is the most distinct smell?

Try creating a scent trail. It could pass a strongly-scented flower, then a delicately fragrant flower. At some point on the trail, you might need to crush a leaf to smell it. Perhaps make your trail pass a muddy patch with a pungent earthy smell.

One of my young colleagues, Poramin Watnakornbuncha, has a habit of travelling with his steam distiller set to collect various plant smells from different places and keep them in bottles. He gives one bottle to the owner of the land, and adds the other to his own collection. It's his way of recording the *sense of place* with the *scent of place*.

Reflect back to a place or an incident in your life. When you recall it, what smell comes to mind?

TASTING
Associated Attribute: Love & forgiveness

Our tongues detect five groups of tastes: sweet, sour, salty, bitter, and umami or savoury, which we call *nua* in Thai. Since mouth and nasal cavities are connected, taste is closely related to smell. Both senses combine to create diversity of food tastes.

The main role of tasting is to identify the substances that the body needs for nourishment. It is that urge for something salty, or something sweet, or something sour, or something that you cannot quite pinpoint, but which you know is exactly what you want when you taste it. I once went on a walkabout along an organic rice field with a traditional Thai medicine man, surveying the wayside meadow plants. I picked up a leaf for him to taste. Although I knew its chemical content and medicinal properties, I did not tell him. The medicine man who had a fine sense of taste could tell me right away that the plant contains iron.

Another friend who works with natural farming and is interested in children's learning process told me that his colleagues in the field of child development and nutrition have noticed there is an emerging trend showing that children who eat food with a wide diversity of tastes are mentally healthier than children who are addicted to processed food, which is mainly sweet and salty, savoury with additives. The latter group are often found to cause depression and panic attacks. More and more evidence shows there is a correlation between tastes, diversity of foods and nutritional balance, or good health. Equally there is growing evidence that consumption of a diet high in Ultra-processed Foods (UPFS) correlates with obesity and negative health outcomes.

Sharing food is an important cornerstone of family life and community care. Taste is therefore a sense that relates to love and care, nourishing each other, wanting to make delicious meal for loved ones, so they may eat well and be strong.

Noticing tastes

We taste food better when we give time and attention to observing each mouthful. After noting the aroma, we then note the first taste that appears. Chew the food well, and notice how the taste changes as we process the food in our mouth. Even after we have swallowed the food, note the aftertaste that emerges or lingers at the end. How many tastes did you get during each step of eating that bite?

Thank the food, the plants and animals that sustain our lives with their own, and thank the people who provide it and nourish us. It's a gift of love in return.

TOUCHING
Associated Attribute: empathy

The sense of touch or tactile sense is a vast category. It includes the physical senses both on our external skin and the internal organs within. It includes acknowledging high and low temperatures, pressures, pains, or textures.

It is the most basic need-to-know sense regarding conditions that are conducive to living, of sensing danger and threats, and recognizing environments that are safe, nourishing and cherishing.

Touch is therefore related to empathy.

Many cultures have practices that use the body to survey the environment for survival. In the dry northeastern region of Thailand known as Isan, Khemthong Morat, AKA Jued, founder of "Dek Rak Pa" (Children Love the Forest) group, told of how he located the spot to dig for water on his land by walking about stark naked at night. The thin, sensitive skin of the genitals is readily aware of the humidity that the earth releases as moist heat in the evening, after it's been baked by the scorching sun all day. It is a traditional wisdom of the Isan people.

"At around midnight to 2 am, I stripped off and walked all over the place. Wherever I felt heat radiating out from the ground, I would mark it with a stick. I walked naked like this for many nights, until I could close my eyes and visualize the pattern of heat radiation of the whole piece of land. Then came the design stage. I sketched out the area to plant a forest, the area to dig a pond, then finally the place to build the house. Shallow underground water absorbs heat all day, then releases it at night. It's particularly easy to feel it in the summer. I learned it from my father's generation, who learned it from their elders way back. In the summer, when there's heat given off at night, that's where there's water underground."

Our skin is the largest organ in our body. It is a bag that protects us and holds so many memories to care for our safety. It remembers love and the warm embrace of a mother, but it also remembers fear. It has a repulsion that pushes us away from whatever is deemed undesirable.

Modern urban denizens have accumulated all kinds of fears regarding contact with nature since they were toddlers. They are trained to fear dirt, and are taught that earth is dirty. They do not want to go bare-foot even on grassy lawns and sandy ground. Swimming can only be done in a clear blue sterilized pool. While it was normal for my generation to learn to swim in rivers, canals, or muddy ponds, it is unthinkable to the new urban dwellers. They find it disgusting.

In fact, our body needs direct contact with the soil. We have known for sometimes now that there are microbes living in the soil that are beneficial to our health. One of the most researched species is the bacteria *Mycobacterium vaccae*, which can be found in all kinds of soil across the globe. Direct skin contact with these bacteria on our skin stimulates our brain to release serotonin, the happy hormone. Not surprisingly, gardening tends to be a therapeutic activity.

Allowing our bare feet to touch the earth regularly is also important for our health. The West calls it 'earthing' or 'grounding'. It has been found to help with the exchange of electric particles. The ground contains a lot of negative ions, which neutralize the positive charge of free radicles that our body has been accumulating throughout the day through our metabolism. It helps maintain our natural immunity.

But what if we fear earth or even grassy lawn? What do we do then?

Stepping out of your comfort zone

I once went camping with a family who had a 6-year-old daughter. The parents wanted the girl to learn about nature, but they seemed to be somewhat afraid of the big wide world outside a building. They were afraid the child might fall over, afraid of accidents, and perhaps also afraid of dirt. The little girl was not familiar with uneven ground. Her balance was not very good.

That afternoon we all went to play in a cool, clear forest stream. All the kids were having a lot of fun, splashing in a pool with a small waterfall. The 6-year-old wanted to join in, but she stayed firmly on the edge of the water, not daring to step in. Every time she was about to try a small step, her parents would call out from the bank, prohibiting her. To ease their worries, I offered to take care of her. I let her explore the new world at her own pace. She squatted down and reached out to touch the flowing water – Whoa! It's cool and it moves! Her eyes lit up with a spark. She tried hitting the water – Splash! Splash! Wow! That was fun! She giggled. When she began to get familiar with the stream water, she started to look further to where the other children were playing and laughing.

She tried taking a small step, and immediately retracted her foot. It didn't feel stable.

So I held her hand and taught her how to take steady steps. At a somewhat challenging point I showed her how we could sit down on the rock and slide forward. We focused on one step at a time, and then she could do it by herself. Yes! Yes! Yes! I was so proud of her.

One way of managing our fear is to go to the edge of our comfort zone, and contemplate the world outside its boundary. Look at it, take time to get to know it, and slowly move out. Our comfort zone will begin to expand.

However, if you have a deeply buried fear, you could try to trace back to where it came from. If it is a bad wound, professional consultation with a therapist might be helpful.

Observing touch and detaching yourself from it

As with other senses, we can improve the ability of our skin to receive information through observation, contemplation, and recording. You can close your eyes and guess the object that a friend places on your skin in the same way that we practice our sense of smell.

If you are repulsed by earthy dirt, you could start with touching things around you. Try touching woody surfaces, and describing what it feels like. Compare that with a metallic surface, then glass, paper and plastic. Now step outside and feel the air. Is it humid, dry, heavy or light? How so? Touch leaves: a smooth waxy leaf, a soft leaf with tiny hairs (beware of stingy plants, of course). Finally when you have got to the point where you are relaxed and centred, when you can accept the natural state of each thing, then you can try touching the soil. What is it like in different places? Is it crumbly, hard, or sticky?

Having a fine tactile sense does not necessarily make us overly sensitive, easily hurt, feel pain acutely or get upset. It can be similar to how we observe the sounds we like and dislike, or our preferences as experienced through our other senses, such as our eyes seeing beauty and ugliness. When we observe with stillness, it is true that we notice a lot, but we receive information as an observer rather than as an affected being. The things that impact us are not personal.

It is not so difficult to learn to be an observer of something that happens at a distance detectable by our senses, but not easy when it is a pain experienced by our physical body. After all, this is the role of pain. It serves as a warning for us to take care of our body, to avoid things that harm us, to find ways to heal

Nonetheless, in the end we cannot really avoid pain. Unless we die instantly in a sudden crash or are lucky enough to die easily in our sleep, most of us are likely to have to face some pain before we can shed our body.

We are not really afraid of death as much as we are afraid of the pain and physical suffering before we die.

In Thailand we are used to the advice given by Buddhist meditators to change our relationship with pain through mindful observation. The practice teaches us to acknowledge painful sensations without allowing them to cause too much suffering. In a nutshell, this means learning to see the pain without becoming the affected person with pain, or at least learn to be able to bear the pain – Ouch! When you are in pain, it is not something you want to hear.

Perhaps it will help to hear this from someone with a direct experience.

When my husband, Job, was about 12-13 years old in the 8th grade, he had a loose tooth and went to a dentist. The tooth had to be pulled out, but for some unknown reason, perhaps to save money, he asked the dentist not to administer any anaesthetic. The dentist's extraction of his tooth was felt to the full – the forceps gripping on the tooth and tearing it away from the attached nerves and blood vessels. Job opened his mind to embrace the pain wholeheartedly, in his words, "to really, really know what it was like". He looked into the immense pain, and it became numb. Throughout the experiment, there was him the observer hovering above, watching the whole saga from the ceiling, looking down on the little boy on stage.

I am certain that the man that boy has grown into would not refuse the anaesthetic today, but that experience showed him how he could watch pain and be detached from his body.

This does not mean you should disconnect your senses from the goings on of the world. Rather, it is a re-arrangement of the relationship between the two in a new way. It is to know the sensation, but not get carried away with the feeling.

MOVING
Associated Attribute: vitality

This group of senses includes balance and coordination between the different parts of the body.

Children who have grown up with the current, modern-day lifestyle show shockingly diminished physical development. They grow up wearing thick cushioned shoes, which they tend to drag with their feet across the smooth, even floors of condominium buildings, hotels, and shopping malls. In addition, they spend so much time with screens, that it is hardly surprising they have problems with balance and coordination. Many have become suspicious of the big wide world beyond the controlled boundaries of modern air-conditioned buildings.

It is not just with the uneven ground in the natural world that they find difficult to cope, even the open wooden stairs of traditional houses in the Thai countryside are daunting. Many urban kids freeze up with them. They're afraid; they're confused; they don't know how to step on them.

I was hardly an athletic kid nor one who excelled at dancing. In fact, my worst grades at school were always for PE. Nonetheless, I was an urban kid who ran barefoot on the lawn, walked across a paddy field to see my grandmother, clambered over rocks at the sea shore, and climbed trees, as did all the other kids at that time. When I became a teenager, I started hiking regularly. It was an activity I did well. My spine, my steps and my breath were in sync and in tune with the mountains. Generally, outside of basketball courts, the way non-athletic kids and athletic kids used their bodies in everyday life was not so different. It was simply because our way of life was not very disconnected from nature.

However, I had never really known the joy that comes with the ability to move one's body at another level until I started to learn belly dancing at the age of over forty. I learned to move my joints in flowing waves like a snake. I learned to isolate the movements of different parts of my body, and coordinate or layer them in synchronization as I wished – at least to a certain degree. I felt comfortable with my body as I allowed it to be a tool to receive and express feelings.

In her book *Grandmother's Secrets*, Rozina-Fawzia Al-Rawi, a Bedouin belly dancer teacher from Baghdad tells of the process her grandmother used to teach her belly dancing.

The first lesson was divided into three steps. On the first day, grandmother gave her a piece of chalk and asked her to draw a dot on a blackboard, gathering all her attention and concentrating all her being into this one dot. She was to draw the dot repeatedly until there were no thoughts left. The dot "is the beginning and the end, the navel of the world", grandmother explained.

The next day, grandmother asked her to draw a vertical line "as long as three dots lying above each other." This is the first Arabic alphabet, the *alif*. Fawzia repeatedly drew the *alif*, over and over again until there was nothing else left in her mind but the straight line of *alif*. She drew until she saw only *alif* in all things: arms, legs, hands, feet, back. They were all reduced into the core shape of *alif*, not unlike a stick man.

"*Alif* is the first expression of the dot. … It is through the dot's longing to grow beyond itself that the *alif* is born. Regardless of their multiple, outer shapes, all letters are the *alif* in their essence.", grandmother explained.

Then on the third day, grandmother finally let her put the piece of chalk down. Instead, she got Fawzia to draw lines in the air with her hips. Start with a balanced stance on both legs, then shift the weight to the right hip, like a pendulum, with the belly button being the pivoting point with a string tying to the moving hips. When it can't move to the right any further, let it swing back to the left. When this movement is drawn on the blackboard as a curved horizontal line, then add a dot underneath, and the second letter in the Arabic alphabet appears, *ba*.

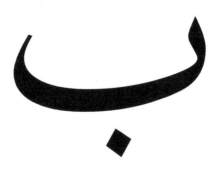

"The dot is the beginning. The dot begets all the other letters. The dot is below and the alif in between: [the letter ba]. Together, they form the word *abb* (father), one of the names of the Divine. When you whirl or when you circle your pelvis, you are drawing the dot, the origins. From this shape all other movements are born – they all stem from this dot, from the navel in your belly."

That was how the origin of universe, god, and grandmother, are all embedded in the centre of Fawzia's body and in all her movements. Even when she remains still, it is an energetic stillness. It is a dot that has not yet expressed itself into a movement. It is still, but not inert, right on the belly button.

Fawzia recounts how she felt that day after her grandmother finished the lesson, "I was excited to know that I carried inside me a source from which everything was born. Time and again, I watched the inward spiral of my navel with respect. Going around with all this power inside my belly made me feel secure and confident."

This is a completely different from how I learned traditional Thai dance as a kid. The teacher was fierce. She walked around with a stick in her hand, ever ready to whack our ankles. She forced my straight fingers to bend backward with force in an attempt to create an ideal Thai dancer's hand. Not surprisingly, I hated Thai dancing classes.

The centre of our body is our pivoting point of balance. If it is strong, our body structure will be strong too. It is the area of the *Tan Tien* in Chinese, or *Hara* in Japanese. It is an important life energy centre.

Our muscles and ligaments also have a memory storing-system called fascia. It is rather like a strong but flexible net covering our muscles, made out of silica, the same element used in a computer to store memories. Not only does it store memories well, it can also transmit information in a flash, at the speed of 30,000 km/sec, or 10% of the speed of light, which is much faster than the nervous system.

Fascia is therefore an important part of physical intelligence. Its role is to ensure that our body movements remain safe and normal. It is a mechanism to protect us from accidents. Without fascia, a movement would be subjected purely to the basic laws of physics. For example, our heads would fly off under a spinning force. Movement under fascia works like a safety belt that reduces the impact from the spin by about 15%.

We can develop our physical intelligence by giving the fascia system more exercise. With more practice, the physical memories become finer and more precise. We won't need to use the brain to take command of everything. It's like a distribution of power, from central control to local authorities, making our body more efficient and in the flow.

When I first tried belly dancing, I was ever so awkward. I am a head-based person, running my life through my brain. I make plans. I needed to see the big picture of the whole dance, before my brain would analyse the movements, breaking it down into sections and small steps. Then I would order my left hip to lift up 1-2-3-4, and so on so forth. The power of decision was totally at the big command centre. A naturally gifted dancer with high physical intelligence would look at me and be totally perplexed, exclaiming, "Why don't you just simply let your leg go."

I swear on the honour of a person who started with limited physical intelligence, and hasn't forgotten the experience – we really can train ourselves.

You don't have to try belly dancing, but I invite you to practice training your feet to see the way.

The Native Americans call it "Fox Walking", and Fawzia's grandmother calls it "Seeing Feet".

Fox Walking

I learned of fox walking through the writing of Jon Young. He is the first white American whom Tom Brown, a Native American tracker, chose as an apprentice, and he relayed Apache knowledge of the wild to him since Young was 12. He was taught to walk like a fox, but never knew why it was called so until one winter morning, when the snow was piled up thickly on the tree branches, and Young was trailing a fox. He watched as the fox walked silently down the tapering skinny branch of a maple sapling which was hanging down low, and dropped itself onto the snowy ground and continued on its way. Nothing else moved. The branch did not move, and the snow remained piled up thickly. Then Young very lightly tapped the branch, and all the snow fell off.

When a fox walks, it doesn't send off any vibration. That's how it is able to hunt.

To practice fox walking, try it out in the following two stages.

Stage One. Close your ears, using your fingers to push down the little flaps in front of the ear cavities. Then walk about as you normally walk, noting the sound and any sensation you receive.

Most people tend to hear the *teung – teung – teung* sound of the heel thumping on the floor. Many feel the vibration from the impact on the floor travelling up to their knees. For some it can go right the way up to their neck. Apart from the fact that our noisy walking would send all the animals fleeing from us, the vibration of the heel impact cannot be that good for the joints in our body.

Stage Two. Try the exercise again, but this time try to find a way of walking quietly without creating physical vibration. Note how the walk is done. Which part of the foot touches the ground first?

This is fox walking. We use the middle part of the foot towards the outer rim to touch the ground first. Then the weight of the body is transferred onto the whole foot.

It is the way indigenous tribal people walk all over the world, be they the Kung bushmen of the Kalahari desert, the aboriginal people of Australia, or the Dara-ang tribe from the hill behind my house in Chiang Dao, Northern Thailand.

When they walk, they barely look down at the ground. They use owl eyes to see the world around them, while their feet detect the ground before stepping fully on it. If there is a thorn, withdraw their foot before transferring their weight onto it. Their balance is maintained since the weight is still held on the back foot, giving enough stability to spring the foot in front away from danger.

As far as I have observed, some modern urban people taught themselves to fox-walk automatically as children, those people who grew up in two-storey wooden houses with formidable elders who tended to take an afternoon nap. If the children wanted to play, which often meant running about, they needed to find ways to do it quietly. It is interesting to watch how these people run: their heads remain parallel to the ground. There is no bouncing up and down, since there is no pounding impact.

Fawzia's grandmother also taught her to walk up and down stairs without looking down. The feet are trained to sense their own way. "Let your feet see for you," she said, "They'll keep you from falling much better than your eyes."

Try wearing shoes and taking shoes off to practice fox-walking. Which is easier?

TOTAL BODY AWARENESS
Associated Attribute: fully alive

In daily life, we sense everything all at once. When we're working, however, many of us tend to be fully concentrated on whatever is in front of us. There are only a few activities that require us to open up all our senses and bring them into use conscientiously.

For me, it is riding a bicycle through chaotic city traffic.

Cycling is the nearest thing to flying that we can do. Our balance is right on, we flow through the world on two wheels, feeling the sun, wind, and rain, while catching a waft of different smells along the way. We can even taste the air. The eyes, of course, are seeing the road, and the ears are hearing the sounds of birds, cars, and passersby. When we cycle on a road that is shaded with trees, studded with flowers, with the sound of a flowing stream alongside, it is pure bliss.

Cycling on a city road busy with cars moving in all directions, however, is another story. It is not a scenario I enjoy much. I often get stressed, with both the noise and exhaust fumes, and certainly stressed with cars and motorbikes that do not respect traffic laws, and regard bicycles as insignificant mosquitoes that they can brush off the road. That is how I had to build an armour to protect myself when I ride in a city like Bangkok. It's an energetic armour that emits a kind of radiation, which has something to do with the confidence of knowing my right to be on the road. It makes cyclists visible to car drivers and accepting us.

Wearing bright red lipstick also helps. Flash a smile and cars often give way.

There are times, however, when my awareness of my surroundings is taken up to another level without much effort. It tends to happen in periods when I cycle in the city a lot and master the art. I see everything. It is normal for city cyclists to use their owl-eyes wide-angle lens, and be able to detect periphery movements from the corners of their eyes, but this more advanced state of awareness allows us to somehow know things that are coming from behind too. In this state, I am able to weave my way through the traffic labyrinth, and flow like a kite caught on a high wind. It is a relaxed state without much tension, but with very fine, acute awareness in every pore of my skin. There is a Kung Fu spirit about it. Like a samurai on a solo journey through a wild land.

In such a state, all our senses are open and awake. It is not an alertness which comes with lurking dangers, which is laced with stress. Rather, it is simply knowing, just receiving information. Many Thai Buddhists may think of the saying *Roo Tua Thua Prom*, literally translated as "whole body ready awareness", which I think is exactly what it is.

Cities like Bangkok can actually be a great field of practice. I am a fast walker. In a shopping area there are groups of people walking and chatting at a leisurely slow pace, stopping intermittently to look at roadside merchandise, and effectively blocking the whole pavement. if this happens when I am in a hurry to get through, I play a game that I call "Siamese Mud Carp Getting Through the Khone Papeng Barrier".

The Khone and Papeng Falls are huge cascades across the Mekong River in southernmost Laos near the Cambodian border. It's not one big, lofty cliff wall like Niagara, but breaks down into several cascades of different sizes and angles in the midst of fierce rapids and whirling pools. Hundreds of species of fish need to migrate through the cascades to lay their eggs up river. The biggest challenge is how to navigate their way through. The Mekong fish are not like salmon who can leap high over rocky cascades, and here the terrain at many points is too high for the fish to leap.

They need to rely on a guide, the Siamese Mud Carp – a tiny carp species not longer than 20 cm. It is a very common freshwater fish living in large schools.

The Siamese Mud Carp uses collective knowledge from the whole school to navigate the route. The fish swimming on the outer rim sense the strongest water current and turn towards it, leading the rest of the fish in the school to follow suit. They keep going until they meet with a dead end, when fish from the other side of the school sense the water current from another direction and take a turn to lead the way. In this fashion, they are able to zig-zag their way through small and large passages, and finally get the whole school over the cascades. The other fish species just simply follow them.

Hence, when I need to get through a crowd on a pavement, I pretend to be a Siamese Mud Carp, looking for a passage through. Sometimes I need to tilt my body left and right to get through without bumping into people and hawkers with charcoal braziers grilling pork or woks of banana fritters full of bubbling hot oil. I get into the state of whole body awareness and flow quickly through.

Nonetheless, kudos for the animal in which this trait is most developed, has to go to the deer. We humans tend to see deer as uber-alert, easily scared animals, like the jumpy big-eyed Bambi. However if you really observe them well, you would see an uber-cool animal, who lives totally in the present. It has excellent hearing, and is ever so quick to detect and flee from predators. But when the moment of lurking danger passes, it shakes off the stress and turns back to grazing at leisure, as if the near fatal moment had never happened. Deer can change their activities very quickly. It is almost always aware of what's going on around it. We can see that from the pricked and twitching ears while it grazes at ease, always ready to move.

In our Shaolin Kungfu class in Bangkok, Shifu or Master Ju teaches us to develop the awareness of our surroundings from the very beginning. We may be concentrating on practicing our kicks, but when we turn around, we must be able to answer in that very second what hand gesture Shifu has just made. Was it hammer, scissors, or paper; with the right or the left hand; or was there no gesture at all? In a test to upgrade our belt level, we test in a group as well as solo. Shifu observes how aware we are of what's going on around us. Does a student slow down to move in sync with others? Is she/he collected enough not to follow a colleague who makes a mistake?

Fine-tuning our basic senses opens up our body to detect subtle energy automatically. When we are in the present, receiving information detected by the senses without any reactive judgement, just simply knowing and contemplating our observations, we begin to be fascinated. We reclaim the fresh heart and clear eyes that see the world with amazement. We regain a sense of wonder.

When things that hit us are not personal – they're just the things we come across, the way we see the world begins to change.

Caroline Myss, the energy therapist who studied the work of Saint Teresa of Avila, compares our different perspectives of the world to a tall building in New York City. Life on the street level is chaotic and raucous. We walk in a hurry and accidentally crash into others; we pass piles of stinking garbage; loud horns sear our ear drums; heat radiating off from the road surface feels like hot air from an oven; but biting into a hot dog while listening to a busking guitarist on the roadside is rather fun. Then as we walk up the stairs, step by step, we begin to see more. Finally, we reach the penthouse. It's breezy and cool. We can see how the roads are connected. Oh! There's a pretty park, and just two blocks away there's a river. It is so near. We could not have known it at the street level.

Scattered pieces of the world we knew from our basic five senses at the ground level begin to take their place in the big picture of the jigsaw puzzle.

Myss calls the world from this penthouse perspective the level of Grace. That's the next chapter.

Chapter 4
Go beyond the realm of the senses

> "They say that when you get old, as I am,
> your body slows down. I don't believe it… I have a
> theory that you do not slow down at all, but that life
> slows down for you. …Everything becomes languid,
> as it were, and you can notice so much more when
> things are in slow motion. The things you see!
> The extraordinary things that happen all around you,
> that you never even suspected before."
> "Take flowers", she said,
> pointing at the blooms that filled the room.
> "Have you heard flowers talking?"
>
> ~ Mrs. Kralefsky in *My Family and Other Animals* by Gerald Durrell

When we slow down and are more receptive, we begin to detect clearly subtler energies within our body, or what is coming into our body. It could be light, fluttering vibrations, flashing flushes, spiral currents, electrifying sensations, dull thuds, or whatever. It is not all that different from other physical sensories, only that it's so fine and subtle you might need to stay still to feel it.

In Thailand, many of us first notice electro-magnetic energy in our body when we learn to practice vipassana meditation. This practice in Theravada Buddhism involves focusing on seeing things as they are, which requires practitioners to observe the world from a state of tranquility and full awareness. In a vipassana class, the teacher guides us to simply observe the sensations that occurs without reacting to them. Just observe whatever happens and then see it disappear. We are urged not to pay much attention to them other than simple acknowledgement.

However, energy sensations can sometime be a language, a signal pattern informing us of something. It varies in different individuals. Each one of us has to figure out our own meaning.

I found out my personal pattern when I was somewhat lost in a snowstorm in Tibet. It was a mid-summer snow storm, in August 1995.

At that time, I had the opportunity to join an expedition to trace an ancient Lama's Guide to a sacred land called Pemako. It describes a location hidden within the folds of the Himalayas around where the River Tsangpo takes a sharp hairpin turn. It entailed a month-long trek on foot to a place believed to be the heart centre of the Goddess Uma. What happened there are stories for another book.

The discovery of my energetic pattern, however, happened on the last day of our trek, when we crossed over a snow-clad pass back to the Tibetan plateau.

Even though there were many of us in the expedition, when we walked, we each went at our own pace, so in effect we tended to walk alone. When we came to a junction, we simply observed the signs made by the person in front of us.

That day there was a heavy snowstorm just when we were crossing over the mountain pass. The wind was whirling snow in all directions, making the air all blurry white, with just about one foot's visibility. I could not hear anything but the whooshing of the wind. All I could do was to place one foot in front of the other in the footsteps of the person in front.

Then I came to a multi-way junction. At that point I had lost my orientation. It was not as simple as an urban crossroads, where one could take a guess of what might be to the left or right. I could not see anything. No one would hear me if I called out. My feet and legs were numb and without sensation. Walking on was driven solely by my willpower alone.

I was by myself in the snowstorm. My basic senses could not detect anything. How should I decide which direction to take?

Stories from my childhood reading the book "Little House on the Prairie" by Laura Ingall Wilder began to swirl in my head: the many tales of people missing their houses on their walk home in snowstorms and freezing to death. I tried to push them away, and focus on the immediate problem: which way do I go?

As the question appeared clearly in my head, the left side of my neck suddenly felt a tingling sensation, so I decided to walk that way. After a short while I bumped into two Tibetans walking quickly from the opposite direction in the storm. I said the name of the village where I needed to go, signaling with my hand for the direction to ask them the way. They nodded in affirmation.

I thought no more of it at the time, merely thinking how lucky I was to have made the right guess.

It was only much later that I started to put the pieces together to make sense of it all when I was playing the Findhorn Foundation's Transformation Game. In the first move of the game, each player needs to intuitively choose the right direction, which I kept getting wrong. I was completely stuck until I suddenly thought of the snowstorm incident. I then asked silently for the right direction to take, and that tingling sensation on one side of my neck appeared again. I followed the sensation, and it was right, and continued to always be right throughout the entire game.

I have since tested this pattern many more times – asking my body to show me the direction to take. May I stress that every time I tested it, it was always in a safe situation, where a mistake would not be of any grave consequence. Sometimes it was in a game. Once I tried it out in the popular party game "Werewolf", where the aim is to identify the werewolf and the witch hiding in the village. If we guess wrong, a member of the community will disappear one by one until there is no one left and the werewolf would win. Halfway through a game, I tried asking my body to identify the witch, and the tingly electrifying sensation indicated a direction where only one active player remained. I successfully pointed out the witch, killed her off, and won the game. Then I felt guilty as if I had cheated. I used witchcraft to kill a witch, so I never did it again.

There was no need for me to test it any more. I had accumulated enough observations to conclude the meaning of electrical sensations in the region of my neck or shoulders when I asked for directions. I became more confident of it when I swapped accounts of the experience with others and found quite a substantial number of people who had felt the same signal. It was not just a figment of my imagination. I am not a weirdo.

I feel a little uncomfortable disclosing this kind of personal information, but it is nothing compared to what I'm about to reveal next.

May I ask readers to suspend judgement for the time being? When you have finished reading the next passages, you can pick it up again.

This sensing of vibrations and subtle electrical currents in the body is at the edge of our ability to receive information through the tangible sensory organs. As I mentioned before in the previous chapter, if we practice detailed observations of the basic senses enough, other subtler senses that are often called the sixth, seventh, or eighth sense, will emerge in their own time, naturally. It comes with being still, centred, fine-tuned, and empty.

It is a state of being that allows us to begin to detect that we are connected to many lines of energy in the universe. Energy that religions refer to as gods. This is a state of being when we use telepathy to communicate with other species, both visible and invisible beings.

Once, around the year 2002, I went hiking at St.Clare Lake in Tasmania with my husband and another friend. That afternoon I felt like walking in a continuous rhythm, as opposed to stopping to look at this and that every few steps, and so I was way ahead of the others on the trail. When we move in flowing pattern, stepping in sync with our breath and the beating of our heart, we tune in to the pulse of the landscape and became one with it.

Then I came across a small clearing in the forest. I stopped and stood there. Suddenly I could feel numerous spirals of energy spinning like minute whirlwinds into my body, and I immediately knew what had happened to the forest at that particular spot.

When I looked around, however, I noticed the tree species and could analyse them from the knowledge I had been accumulating before I got to Tasmania and from what I had recently learned from my local naturalist friend. This knowledge took me to the same conclusion about what had happened. I knew where a big tree had fallen in a storm, causing sunlight to shine from a certain direction. Light-loving trees of different species had subsequently grown up at the spots I saw. It had happened many years back and the fallen tree was no longer there. Only big new trees had grown up in its place, with a small clearing remained where the tree branches were competing to take over. It was a common succession story that happens in forests all the time. There wasn't anything particularly unusual. What was strange was the way I took in information in a forest I was totally unfamiliar with.

This created a serious doubt concerning my experience of seemingly receiving an instant download of information. Perhaps what I really experienced was simply effortless information processing from accumulated knowledge when I was in a state of total relaxation.

However, there have been other times when I have been still enough to notice an idea dropping into the centre of my head.

An idea that came from outside and was not my idea.

Yogis recognize that humans have five body layers on different levels. The diagram we see depicted in books tends to show layers of these bodies like Russian dolls, but it is not layered like an onion. Rather, the different bodies permeate and fuse with one another, each with varying density. The tangible physical body that we can touch with our hands is the densest, followed by the finer energy bodies culminating in the very finest.

Science is beginning to explain this. At the quantum level, we are both energy wavelengths and particles at the same time, so it is not at all odd that information and matter should flow and interact with one another.

There is an elementary exercise that we can practice to see subtle energetic bodies. The easiest to see is the zone around the edge of our physical body. It is part of our aura. Find a white wall or simply a sheet of white paper, raise your hands against that white background and look at the air around the fingers or the whole hand with somewhat blurry eyes. Do not focus on the flesh. You will begin to see diffusing pale-coloured light around the edges. Explore this further. Try connecting the fingers of both hands then pulling them apart, pull in and out, further and nearer repeatedly. Can you see the energy field between the fingers of your two hands? It may appear as streams of lights, like pulling nougat.

I choose this exercise to provide tangible evidence that many of us may share a similar experience at the same time, and see together to some extent how we are composed of energetic subtle bodies. Each person will have to use their own tools that are not basic sensory organs to verify this phenomenon. There isn't a common tool like a microscope for us to prove what we see and share the experience.

This is the major hurdle in trying to talk about non-tangible things that cannot be seen with the eyes, heard by the ears, or touched with the hands. Not only do we hardly have the vocabulary in human language to discuss such topics, but words that are commonly used can not communicate what we really want to say, as they are full of other meanings connected to spiritual practices in particular cultures.

Take for instance the Thai word *Saksit*. The nearest common translation in English is 'sacred'.

The word is often used in a holy context, be it a ceremony, an object, or a place.

However, if you look it up in a Thai dictionary, you will see the meaning described as "An object or a state with super-natural power, able to grant a wish. Has magical power".

Some of my friends dislike this word immensely. They do not like the pairing of *Sak* – high status, and *Sit* – rights. It has connotations of a culture of authoritarianism. It implies the setting of something or somebody having a higher status than others, with rights over them. The word is rooted in an unequal class-based society.

Yet, to me, *saksit* is more akin to the original meaning of 'sacred'. It speaks of a value worthy of respect. There is a certain quality of something pure, genuine and of integrity, that may not be violated. It is the old meaning before the religious establishment took the word to use for ceremonies, and it thereby became a religious word.

For me then, life is sacred. Mountains are sacred. Rivers are sacred. The land and the seas are sacred. These are my temples.

Apart from the limitations posed by language, the fact that we live in a society that does not accept unprovable phenomenon is a further barrier to talking about it. We may be broad-minded people who are well aware of the limitations of science, knowing that there are many more things which science cannot prove, yet we do not want to be obsessed with it. We are afraid of becoming delusional.

On the other side of the coin, in a society where 'supernatural' phenomena are not viewed as normal events, there tends to be a special admiration and awe for certain spiritual leaders who seem to have highly tuned intuitions and other paranormal abilities. They are regarded as very high-level dharma practitioners, who must be much more highly developed than regular people. This can lead to con schemes, which attract money, worshippers, or trendy new-age types floating on cloud nine, to the extent that many of us are irritated and want to keep a good distance. This means that even when we do have a direct unexplainable experience, we prefer to brush it off. We don't want to think too much of it. We don't want to boast of spiritual experience. We want to stand fully on our own two feet, and be grounded.

The fear, the apprehension, the skepticism, were (and probably still are) obstacles to my own learning. I have not allowed myself to learn to be receptive to the world around me through the fine, subtle tools in my body, even though I have had many direct experiences.

I am pretty sure I am not the only one. We are probably the only generation of people in human history to deny the existence of invisible beings around us, although it is hardly surprising that we are influenced by the values of the age in which we live in, an age that is cautious and uncomfortable with the paranormal.

What would it be like though, if people in general could access the human potential to connect with all things in the universe? What if such connections became the norm? There would be no 'supernatural', only the subtle nature in detail. After all, supernatural simply means very natural.

Would the marketing power of fake mediums (a real problem in Thailand) and fake gurus be significantly lessened, when more or less everyone could access information from nature.

I would like to invite you to explore your own capacities in this area, which I am confident we all have and which can be trained to achieve similar skills as those of our ancestors.

I would like to make a disclaimer here. I am not a highly skilled expert in the craft. I need a lot more practice. There are many people who can teach such skills better than I can, so the book is not designed to be a handbook. It is just a way of sharing and exchanging experiences and an elementary understanding of the bigger picture as far as I can see it now. It is essentially an attempt to open up a conversation.

When we receive information from nature, the first thing we must learn is to hone our discernment, to recognize whether it is in fact a figment of our imagination influenced by our prejudices or projected emotions from our past experiences, or whether it really is a message from others out there. We have to observe our thoughts and see how we listen. We can start by observing how we listen to our friends. How do we react in response? At which point do we feel emotionally involved? Why is that? Do we have additional thoughts thereafter? How much are we interpreting things ourselves?

The art of listening requires a lot of practice. Nowadays there are even specially designed course on deep listening that you can take.

Another area to observe is our own body. How does it respond, both inside and outside when you receive information?

At this point we can actually use a scientific approach to help us learn.

Let's imagine we are explorers on an expedition to a new found land, and we are very honest scientists. We see many new things. We don't yet know what they are, what they mean, but we have to send a report home. What do we do?

We observe and describe our findings in as detailed a way as we can in our journals, don't we? This is the first step in an attempt to get to know something new. We don't jump ahead to interpret what we see. Just observe and describe. Do not analyse. Do not judge.

When we do this often enough, we eventually begin to see a pattern. We might begin to have a posit of what it is, but there is no rush to judge. We continue to gather samples to have better statistics, until the pattern becomes much clearer, and we finally understand its meaning.

This is the most basic observable science.

More importantly, an act of simply observing without trying to make any sense of what we record helps free us from being in an analytical mode, which tends to keep our mind busy with thoughts in the beta wavelength. It takes us to an emptier state of mind like an empty vessel, readily able to receive subtle information and energy from nature.

When I first consciously made myself observe these thoughts, I also asked my body for confirmation as to whether it was information from nature outside me or not. If there was an electrical vibration on top of my head, it tended to mean "yes".

For me, the basic senses give me a map of the world around me, and the subtle vibrations felt in my body serve as a compass, taking me to knowledge from an invisible complex wiring network beyond the realm of the physical body.

It gets easier with practice to discern information coming in from outside versus that of our own imaginative thoughts. When the pattern became more apparent, the need to double-check with the electrical vibration on my body was less. I could recognize when information was being downloaded into me. I began to cross the border from the realm of the physical senses to the realm of the subtle energy of the universe.

According to the art and science of yoga, we can access the original source of the life force by aligning the bodies we have, from the densest to the most subtle, so that energy flows and all is connected. It is the same in Tai Chi and Kungfu. The arrangement of the physical body is therefore important, as it is the basic structure that coordinates with the breath and internal chi flow.

Standing grounded, rooted deeply into the centre of gravity of the earth, while shooting for the sky through the upward line of the backbone through the top of our heads, is the blueprint that serves as the principal foundation of all the arts that use the physical body as a tool for spiritual development in many cultures worldwide.

I have had two friends who move beautifully like nature itself, not unlike an elegant wild animal. One was a school classmate, the other was a college friend. They both moved in sync with nature's rhythm, like a wave washing up on the seashore. Whether they were moving fast, or had even fallen into a rugby scrum, their movements appeared to be in a slow motion. Their bodies seem somehow at one with the surrounding elements, with the light, the soil, the water and the air.

The only word that aptly describe them is *graceful*. It is not, however, the same as the graceful elegant manner that ladies used to be trained to sit, stand, and walk with long skirts trailing. Rather, it is a flowing elegance that is so much more natural.

The grace in my friends' gracefulness is the quality that the Catholics refer to.

We are all familiar with the song "Amazing Grace". In religious terms it is something along the lines of an incredibly wonderful blessing from God.

The lyric speaks of a situation when singer's spirit had sunk to its lowest point, when a miraculous blessing from God appeared and saved that person's life. In this context, the experience of a similar situation recounted by John Mccarthy in his book *Some Other Rainbow* is very interesting. The British journalist was held hostage for 5 years by an Islamic Jihadist group in Lebanon during 1986-1991. The memoir of that experience was co-written with Jill Morrell, his then girlfriend, who campaigned hard to pressure the British government to negotiate to bring Mccarthy and other hostages home. John was not religious but he recalled an incident which occurred in his cell when his spirit had fallen into such a dark place that it was about to break into pieces. All of a sudden a force like a bright light came down and enveloped him and picked him up. He understood immediately that it was Grace.

I have come across several stories of encounters with Grace similar to this, so it seems one has to be almost in a state of breakdown to find it. I also wonder what Christian Grace is in the world of Buddhism. What I have gathered from spiritual practitioners who are interested in inter-cultural communication, such as Caroline Myss and Sadhguru, is that Grace is *siva* in Sanskrit, meaning life force or what the Chinese call *chi*.

The Indian yogi, Sadhguru, explains in his book *Inner Engineering* that:

"Grace is shi-va, literally meaning 'that which is not'. Everything that is has come from 'that which is not'. If you look up at the sky, you will see many stars and celestial objects, but still the biggest presence out there is a vast emptiness. It is in the lap of this no-thingness that the dance of creation is happening right now. This emptiness, which is the basis of creation, is referred to as 'shi-va'."

We feel the presence of this force when we do tai chi. We experience that emptiness within atoms and the fine shimmering vibration in that space when we do vipassana meditation. When we are connected to this same force in all things on earth and the universe, we no longer feel disconnected. We are all in the same energy field of God, that is Grace.

However, Grace that the Christians talk about as a ray of blessed light that revives a broken spirit is probably a particularly concentrated life force, much more so than the regular *chi* we feel on a daily basis.

I sell rose water distilled from my home-grown organic roses, so I would like to compare Grace to the essential oil extracted from flowers. It is a pure essential oil. However, when we extract it, we do not crush the flowers to squeeze out the oil. We have to distill it by passing hot steam through masses of petals, then cooling down the steam, which is condensed into water droplets mixed with essential oil. If we collect a large enough quantity of this mixture, a layer of oil begins to form, floating on top of the distilled water. The oil is then collected and sold as expensive pure essential oil. The remaining distilled product is called 'hydrosol'. It is distilled water tainted with essential oil, or what we call 'rose water'. The regular flowing *pran* or *chi* or life force, is likely to be similar to the rose water. Spray it on the face to feel refreshed, but the medicinal property is really from the essential oil.

Grace is therefore the original source of our essential life force.

We do not need to be in a broken state to access that original force, we can access it when we are in an empty state, where pranic force flows freely.

This does not mean we have to be highly spiritual attained people. We simply need to put aside temporarily our prejudices, worries, self-centred concerns, our thinking, analytical state of mind. Put them down like we put down a rucksack full of stuff.

To borrow Caroline Myss's high rise building metaphor mentioned in the previous chapter, this is akin to depositing luggage at a counter on the ground floor, then walking upstairs, or some might take an elevator, to the upper floors of the human building, up to the zone of Grace.

Just for a while.

My two friends who move so gracefully like waves washing ashore, are both good natured amiable people. I suspect they had been connected to grace through their bodies from a young age.

They move in sync with the rhythms of natural force, just like wild animals do. Is it possible that perhaps most animals are also connected to Grace – to the original source of power?

Could Grace be the universal realm where the lives of different species connect?

Chapter 4 – Go beyond the realm of the senses

Chapter 5
Access the wild wisdom

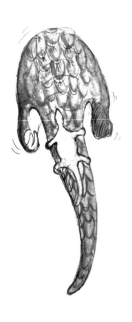

> "Animals too have cognitions, wisdom, abstract thoughts. They know as human do, but they cannot speak out"
>
> ~ Mun Puritatto, a Thai Buddhist monk

One day, in my early primary school years, I came home from school and told my mother that the teacher said there should not be mosquitoes in the world, because they are totally useless and are a real nuisance.

My mother was furious. She answered sharply, "Not everything exists to benefit humans".

Many people seem to think I have all this natural history knowledge because my mother taught me. The truth is, we were not taught facts. When my siblings and I were little, there were no books on nature in Thailand as there are now. The best we had was an encyclopedia featuring wildlife in foreign lands, which we listened to as bedtime stories. We didn't have much factual knowledge, but we absorbed the way our mother looked at the world around her. She would open the front door, and immediately find lots of friends. Some day it was a new bloom, another day it was a butterfly. She would smile and greet them. Once there was a bright green Oriental Whipsnake trying hard to scare us with its wide-open mouth, which unfortunately appeared completely toothless and not at all scary. My mother laughed so hard, the snake looked at her with injured dignity before disappearing into a bush.

She taught us to look at the world around us with their perspectives, so we would have empathy, and be in awe of how cool they were. She would not let us see the world with humans as the centre of the universe.

Given such an upbringing, I get frustrated when I hear someone degrade wild animals, describing at length how lowdown they are on the stairway of evolution – how they lack consciousness, or how they are not smart like humans. Their lives are all about feeding, excreting, copulating, and sleeping. They have no morals, no culture, no capacity to develop their heart and mind as human do. We, *Homo sapiens*, can train ourselves to become noble. We can become enlightened beings.

I do not have any insight into the capacity of animals' minds. I don't know whether they are capable of attaining nirvana or not. Frankly I am not interested in such debates. I don't know enough about nirvana, nor do I know enough about animals. I suspect that the people who devalue animals hardly know anything about them at all. What I am certain of is animals do have consciousness and capacity to develop their mind, at least in many species.

Consciousness is a self-aware cognitive mind that senses and receives certain information, which can be considered from many different dimensions. Some people argue that Artificial Intelligence or AI can also receive information and even be able to express feelings. The point was much discussed in public when Lamda AI from Google said it was afraid to be unplugged. I personally think the incident only reflected that AI had learned to express itself like a human. It arose from a vast pool of data and verbal expressions concerning possible human responses. There is nothing to say that it was a real emotion. The incident did nothing to prove that AI had consciousness.

Many different species have the ability to detect and receive information that humans cannot. We do not see heat imagery the way snakes can. We do not see the patterns and colours of flowers the way birds and bees who see ultra-violet light do. We do not hear the sounds that whales hear. We do not know the world in the same way that plants do. The world that we perceive appears different from the world sensed by other beings. We may be aware of many things they are not, but some of the things we are aware of are not limited to our species as some may presume. Take self awareness as individuals for instance. If animals are not self-aware, why would they struggle to survive? We are not the only animal who knows how to make plans and use tools. In making judgements on the lives of other species, we humans often make the mistake of using our own measurement scale to assess advances in development.

I have a limited understanding regarding the topic of spiritual development, but I am confident that humans are not the ultimate final product of evolution intended by God. Everything that has happened on this planet over the past billions of years has not happened with the objective of creating humans. The systems capable of supporting life on earth was not developed just so that precious human beings could be reborn and ultimately become enlightened, closing the curtain of the universe's greatest show that began with the Big Bang.

If culture means different behavioural patterns among the same living species, then we have to concede that many animals do have culture. The more we study other animals, the more we find this phenomenon.

Different cultures are found in different populations of the same whale species, for instance. Those living in different areas have different dialects and tones from one another, so we can tell if a group of sperm whales is from the Caribbean, rather than the Mediterranean, because their clicking pattern is different. As far as we know, blue whales have at least nine local dialects, and their songs get influenced and changed when they come in contact with another song culture. The clearest example, however, is the orcas. Each community has a very different culture even when they live in the same area. The differences range from vastly different dialects, characters, right down to the food they eat. Without seeing them, you might think they were totally different species. One group eats fish and stays in one area throughout the year, another group eats seals and travels across the ocean.

A study of whale brains has found they have a part of the brain known as paralimbic, which we do not have. It is a part that has something to do with emotion, making their lives in this dimension highly complex. Whales do not only have awareness of individuals, they also have a sense of community connection at a level beyond other animals, humans included.

Once I went on a Bryde's Whale watching trip in the Gulf of Thailand. We saw nine whales altogether that day. Three whales swam after our boat when we were heading back home, so we stopped the engine, sat on the roof to watch the sunset with them. The whales circled around us in a leisurely fashion. We all felt a chain of connection, some kind of friendship that they were offering us.

Anyone who reads wildlife news regularly will recall reports of unexpected behaviour by whales and dolphins from time to time. In the past decade, for example, there have been several sightings of hump-backed whales rescuing seals from orcas. In some cases, the seal was being thrown about, as orcas tend to play with their food before eating – a scene that we have seen in David Attenborough's BBC documentary. The hump-backed whale intervened, using its huge fin to scoop the seal up onto its back before carrying it away to a safe place.

This was not an isolated incident as such acts have been observed so many times that they have been reported in academic papers.

Hump-backed whales gain nothing from saving the lives of seals. Seals cannot repay them in any way in the future, yet the whales still rescue them. The behaviour occurs so frequently that we could perhaps call it a culture.

It is possible that chasing away orcas is no big deal for such giants as hump-backed whales. Perhaps they are already used to protecting their calves from orcas and helping out seals from time to time requires little effort.

Who says animals have no consciousness and concern for other species as humans do? Who says animals do not help one another altruistically, without getting benefits in return, personally or for family members?

Biologists began to recognize animal cultures from the 1950s onwards, when a Japanese primatologist, Kinji Imanishi, observed a group of snow monkeys on Kojima island. This group was unlike any other groups of snow monkeys anywhere else. Here, they would wash sweet potatoes in the sea before eating them. It was particularly fortunate that Imanishi and colleagues got to witness the beginning of this phenomenon. The trendsetter was a monkey named Imo. Several individuals soon followed, and not too long after the whole pack was doing it.

It became a community culture.

The story is the origin of the "Hundredth Monkey Effect" theory, which is used to explain behavioural changes in a given society. The hundredth monkey that washes the sweet potato symbolizes the critical mass that triggers the change. It is the number needed for a small group of people to gain enough influence to shift the norms of the society.

Although there have been many studies of primate cultures worldwide thereafter, academia did not really pay much attention to animal culture till we were nearly approaching the 21st century. Then evidence from almost all groups of animals starting coming forth, including among fish, birds, and even insects.

When I was thinking of writing about animal culture beyond eating, excrementing, copulating, and sleeping, so many examples of all kinds of animals came to mind. There's stories of octopuses, wild boars, elephants, of course, and crows. But I prefer to use examples of animals close to us, so we can easily connect with our own personal experience.

I want to talk about dogs, both domesticated and wild.

I had a dog called Kai Tom. She was a homeless dog born in a temple near my husband's office in Bangkok. We adopted her together with her sister, Kai Jiew. Kai Jiew liked to bully Kai Tom. She really acted as the top dog, and would take Kai Tom's share of food, toys, or our attention. When she didn't get what she wanted, she would snarl at her little sister. Kai Tom never reacted back. She let Kai Jiew have her way, simply walking away from potential conflicts.

I always thought Kai Tom was the underdog, who submitted to Kai Jiew out of fear.

Little did I know. I was totally wrong.

One day, after both Kai Tom and Kai Jiew had been with us for some years, we brought a new puppy home – a Labrador named Mie Khow. Kai Jiew immediately started to go for the little pup to show who was the big alpha, but Kai Tom intercepted her. She stood her ground in front of the puppy and snarled one word at Kai Jiew, who then backed off in surprise.

Kai Tom took care of Mie Khow from that day onwards. Kai Jiew stopped trying to bully Mie Khow long before he grew up to be a much bigger dog than her. Gentle Kai Tom, that quiet dog, who preferred solitude to social drama, stood up and dealt with Kai Jiew, the bully, when a little puppy was threatened, but she never fought for herself.

That was how Mie Khow came to really love Kai Tom, and saw her as his second mother.

The dogs showed their characters clearly the day we moved to a bigger house with more ground for the dogs to run around in. As soon as they were let out of the car, Kai Jiew was overcome with fear of the hitherto unknown place. She stayed where people were, all shaken and curled up in the kitchen corner. Meanwhile, Kai Tom and Mie Khow were excited and happy to run around exploring every nook and cranny of the new place.

It turned out that the bullying Kai Jiew was the most cowardly dog of the pack.

Kai Tom had a remarkably pleasant temperament, which was almost poetic. She liked to lie on the front patio, looking at the sky and floating clouds. Her eyes were so dreamy, that I could not help but think she was an imaginative dog.

We might say that's how pet dogs are. They are close to people, so they become individuals like humans, but it must be different with wild dogs.

That's only because we don't know them.

Let me introduce you to Wolf No.21.

The account given here is from Carl Safina's beautiful book, *Beyond Words: What Animals Think and Feel.* He is a famed ecologist who pioneered ocean conservation.

Safina tells the story through the experience of Rick McIntyre, a zoologist who has been observing wolves in Yellow Stone National Park since they were re-introduced back to the wild in 1995, after the original population was killed by humans and had disappeared entirely from the park for 70 years.

He called wolf No.21, which he observed closely everyday throughout its life, a "perfect wolf".

Twenty-one was a sturdily built male. His broad shoulders could be identified from afar. He was both strong and agile. He never lost in any fight, not even when he battled a pack of six wolves all at once. McIntyre said he fought like Bruce Lee in the movies.

"Watching him felt like seeing something that looked supernatural", he elaborates, "It was like watching Muhammed Ali or Michael Jordan – a one-of-a-kind talent at the top of his game, the extreme high end of the skill set, talent outside of 'normal'." Safina adds "And normal for a wolf isn't like average for a human, because every wolf is a professional althlete."

Not only did Twenty-one never lose a fight, not even once, he also never killed a loser.

He really was a super wolf.

Twenty-one was the first generation of wolf pups born in Yellowstone National Park after their re-introduction. At the time the place was teeming with elks, who had overgrazed the vegetation to the point of degradation, leading to severe land erosion and collapsed waterways, because there had been no large predators like wolves to control the elk population and their behaviour for decades. By the time Twenty-one was two and a half-year's old, he left his birth family and seamlessly took on the alpha position of a small wolf pack whose alpha male had just been shot dead two days before.

His family expanded at an extraordinary fast rate. Normally, only the large alpha female breeds. In this case, however, very soon after Twenty-one came to lead the pack, three she-wolves gave birth at the same time, until the pack grew to have 37 members, which was totally unheard of. It reflected the unusual abundance of food, i.e. the unusually large elk population.

It is not an easy matter to govern 37 wolves, since they always tend to have conflicts with one another. Yet, Twenty-one managed it.

Not only did he control the conflicts among 37 wolves living together, he also took on wolves from other packs.

Wolves are among those animals that can fight each other to the death, as do humans and chimpanzees. They fight over territories and resources similarly to human tribal wars. A favourite strategy is to attack the alpha of the competing pack, because if they can overcome him, it's a victory.

As mentioned, Twenty-one always won the fights, but never killed the losers. He always stopped and let them run away. He was a generous general. He was a big-hearted warrior. It is probably difficult to understand why he did that. Why did he have compassion for his enemies?

It was this kind of behaviour, however, that gave him a strength of character that we call *baramee* in Thai (a bit like charisma). It commands a natural respect in a similar way that Mahatma Gandhi and Nelson Mandela did, but that the ultra-cruel leaders like Adolf Hitler, Stalin, and Mao Zedong did not have. Those men ruled through fear.

We may be impressed with strength, but we remember kindness.

Twenty-one had a quiet confidence. He was elegant and gentle. He knew how to hold back against his enemies or the weaker wolves. When he played with the pups in his pack, Twenty-one would wrestle with them and pretend to lose, so the pups would be glad to win.

He had always been like this since he was a pup himself. The things about him that McIntyre loved the most, was the way Twenty-one took care of his relatives before he left his birth pack. When he got food, he would bring it back to share with those siblings who did not take part in the hunt. He would look out for the weakest in the pack, the ones that tended to get bullied. He would seek them out, take care of them and play with them.

Twenty-one was one of the few wolves living in the wild who died naturally at an old age.

That day, while his family was rolling about and playing together, an elk walked past. Every wolf leapt to its feet and chased after the deer. Twenty-one stood up, looked at the chase for a brief period, then turned in the opposite direction. He walked alone across the valley.

He knew that it was his time. He gathered the very last bit of his strength to hike up the mountain, to the meadow where he and his family used to gather, running around with the pups. A big shady tree grew there. This was where Twenty-one curled up and lay down to sleep for the last time.

He was nine years old. It seems that he had control of his life destiny to the very last day.

That day, McIntyre and his colleagues, all grown-up research scientists, broke down in tears.

If we watch animals or different groups of people closely, in time we will see individuals within the group. Each one, each person, is both alike and different.

I remember well when I first went to study in England at the age of

14 in the 1970s. The human world was not as connected as it is now, and I was confused with the western faces around me. I could not remember them. They all looked the same. I wrote about it in my English essay. The English teacher liked it so much, she called me to her study and encouraged me to observe and record these personal perspectives and early impressions. She saw it as a lesson for everyone to share, because white people also saw other races in the same way. We all looked the same. They could not see individuals either.

The same goes for animals, plants, and fungi.

Let's admit that we do not know the residents of different species on earth very well. All those who make declarations about their inferior intelligence, their lower consciousness, their lack of creativity, a thinking brain, or the need to pause for reflection. How do we know? Where did the information come from, or is it something that we have heard and just passed on as a mindless saying?

The word *derajchan* in Thai, which we use for non-human animals, has a derogatory connotation of lower, uncivilized beings. However, its origin is *tiryag-jati* in Sanskrit, literally translated as "horizontal goers", meaning animals whose bodies run parallel to the horizontal plane of the earth. Their hearts and vital organs are hence protected between their legs. That is as much as we really know, and that definition should suffice.

Humans, on the other hand, stand on two legs, exposing our hearts and vital organs to the big wide world.

That is our challenge. Are we willing to use that open heart? It is an important tool for inter-species communication. It is the window to the healing of our disconnected, nature-deficit syndromes.

Chapter 6
Communicating across species

> "Some people talk to animals.
> Not many listen though. That's the problem."
> ~ Winnie the Pooh, by A.A. Milne

When I was a kid, stories from distant lands and other cultures were full of talking animals and plants. They were the regular roadside creatures that the protagonists met, not fantastic beasts from a magical realm beyond a rabbit hole that Alice fell through. Some stories even began with "Once upon a time when people could still talk to animals…."

Those of us who have grown up in a modern society may see them as just fun stories to entertain children. But even today we can find that there are still some hunter-gatherer tribes who do actually talk to plants and animals.

The Inupiat of Alaska have a culture that is tied up intricately with whales. The relationship there between humans and whales is so much more than simply that of hunters and prey. They can actually talk and exchange information.

In 1986, Harry Brower Sr., a 61-year-old Inupiat, received a message from a young bowhead whale who lived around his hometown 1,000 miles away from where he was in hospital. It told Harry how his mother had been harpooned to death by a group of men. The whale saw all the faces of his mother's killers, which included Brower's own son. Upon investigation, it turned out that the incident really did happen. Scientists then decided to go and learn about the lives of whales from this tribe in order to improve their conservation efforts.

Today, if we talk to people who act as wildlife interpreters, one of the first names to come up is that of Anna Breytenbach. She is probably the world's most famous animal communicator. More precisely, she is an interspecies communicator, for she can talk to both animals and plants. Her work, however, tends to involve animals. She is from South Africa, a land that still has rich arrays of wildlife. Inevitably, conflicts between humans and wild animals frequently occur.

Anna Breytenbach graduated in Psychology, Marketing and Economics from the University of Cape Town, and went on to work as an information analyst in Silicon Valley. However, she had always liked wildlife, and used to volunteer at a cheetah conservation project in her early 20s, so when she moved to work in the United States, she went to learn tracking in her spare time with Jon Young, who in turn had learned it from his Apache mentor since he was a kid. As she did not know the tracks and behaviour of American wildlife as she did the African animals, Jon suggested she tap into her internal feelings. That was when she started to discover the other skills she could use to access information on wild animals.

I learned of Anna Breytenbach from a powerful documentary *The Animal Communicator*, presented by Swati Thiyagarajan, an Indian conservation journalist in South Africa, who was also a co-producer and the director of this documentary.

Swati raised questions gently on behalf of the audience – every doubt, every skepticism. She presented all kinds of situation to test Anna. Meanwhile she witnessed how Anna could walk at ease among a group of reputedly very aggressive baboons, or how Anna could give the correct information about animals with odd behaviours, without any previous knowledge of their backgrounds, be it the case of the Capuchin monkey who was once used as a laboratory testing animal, or the case of the depressed parrot. In the monkey's case, Anna could tell that it had been pinned down by all four limbs and had had its abdomen cut open, even though the scar was covered with thick fur and could not be seen. She could also tell how bonded the parrot had been to the human who raised it, but who had gone away and left it behind. It missed him deeply (and eventually died of a broken heart). Swati heard how Anna was able to give accurate details about the animals she talked to. She followed while Anna tracked wildlife without bending down to analyse footprints or other physical signs. She simply closed her eyes to listen internally and walked across an open plain to find them. Yet even so, Swati was not entirely, totally convinced.

Swati Thiyagarajan is like you and me who grow up analyzing facts, using evidence, logic and reason. Deep down, she still needed a proof that would clear up any shred of remaining doubt.

The opportunity came when Swati met Jurg and Karen Olsen, the couple who founded Jukani Wildlife Sanctuary to give a good home to big cats who had been captured and caged in poor quality zoos all over the world, or from hunting farms that catered to rich, game hunters.

Jurg had always got on well with big cats. He could get close to them and take care of them in a way few people could. Even so, he had a problem with a black leopard called Diablo, who came from a zoo in Europe.

This black leopard would not let anyone near the enclosure fence without snarling. He had had a bad experience with humans and he did not trust them. Jurg had never met a cat that was always so angry and hated humans as much as this one.

There was a large area of grassy field and trees within the enclosure, yet the leopard had never gone out to take a stroll throughout the whole six months it had been there. It remained hiding in the night shade all the time.

Jurg himself got bitten, so badly he was hospitalized for over a week.

Swati then had an idea. She wanted Anna to try talking to the black leopard. It would be the ultimate test. If Anna could talk to it and fix its behaviour, then there would be no further question. Swati would believe whole-heartedly, absolutely, without any doubt, that Anna really could talk to animals. In fact, this would not only be proof of a genuine interpreter, it would be a showcase of skill in inter-species diplomacy.

Swati took a long time to lobby Jurg. Not only did he not believe people could talk to animals like that, he was also wary of a potential accident. This was a fierce, dangerous animal.

Finally, however, he let Swati bring Anna in without telling her anything of its background.

The black leopard lay quiet and still when Anna approached and sat down by the fence near the night shade. It had never relaxed like this with any human before. Both of them – the black cat and Anna – looked at one another in silence, conversing through telepathy. Anna then relayed the conversation to Jurg, Karen, and Swati.

Chapter 6 – Communicating across species 93

"This beautiful black leopard that you asked me to communicate with, it's very over-awed by his new surroundings, having come from a very cramped and stressful place for him. This place has been provided for him, but he's been conditioned by a very unfortunate past. He doesn't want much to do with humans as a result"

"He's immensely powerful. Not just physically which you well know and respect, but he's immensely powerful with wisdom and energetic presence and personality that is far bigger than anyone has ever appreciated about him before, and he commands a certain amount of respect for that. Not in a needy way, but really just by virtue of who he is as a being. There's a very particular thing about his name Diablo. He wants that name changed, because he doesn't like the associations with it, the blackness, the darkness, the diabolical."

Anna then added,

"When asking about his past before coming here, he shows concern about two young cubs that were next to him. He's asking what happened to them"

Throughout the exchange, Jurg did not believe Anna at all. He thought the talk of powerful animal wanting recognition for its true value, etc., etc., was something any con-person could come up with. To guess that it was once harmed by humans was also not difficult. But when Anna asked about the two leopard cubs in an adjacent cage in the European 300, Jurg knew immediately that Anna was real. He and Karen had forgotten about the two leopard cubs entirely. He never told anyone about it, so there was no way Anna could have known from anyone else. It was far too specific.

Anna added further that when she told the black leopard that no one here expected him to do anything, there was no performance, no show, he could just be himself however he wanted, the leopard was relieved. He suddenly began to show an interest and was wanting to explore the place as his natural curiosity took over.

That afternoon the black leopard came out of his night shade and walked about, exploring the outdoor world within the enclosure for the first time since he arrived here six months ago.

Jurg and Anna agreed to change his name to "Spirit". When Jurg went out to see him relaxing in the open grassland that afternoon, the black leopard looked at him calmly. Jurg then tried to talk to him, called him by the new name, and told him that the two leopard cubs were safe and well.

Then suddenly Jurg blurted out with great emotion, "Wow! You're beautiful".

The black leopard cried "owwe"

Jurg talked on, showing his appreciation of the leopard, and it cried "owwe" back 19 times in total.

This was the first time the black leopard was relaxed with Jurg, and he felt comfortable with it too. He felt the leopard understood him.

When Anna returned in the evening, Spirit the black leopard told her that it was the first time a human had truly appreciated him, which took him by surprise. He described it like a wall of appreciation moving towards him. He was so relieved that no one was making demands on him here. The cry "owwe" was a thank you. When Jurg thanked him, he thanked Jurg back, back and forth, back and forth, "Owwe, owwe, owwe"

Jurg was so overwhelmed. He needed to excuse himself from filming.

From the fierce, devilish Diablo to relaxed and dignified Spirit, it became a totally different leopard in one day.

Anna spoke of the difficulty of being a bridge between animals and human. It is painful. She sees both points of view, and the pictures do not match. They are like entirely different movies.

The coastal baboons in Cape Town that Anna relaxed with at the beginning of the documentary were reputed to be very aggressive. They attacked tourists – jumping on them and ransacking cars. They pleaded with Anna, hoping that the humans would understand them as they really were. There was sadness and confusion among the baboon community. They could not understand how the humans could totally misunderstand them to such an extent.

The conflict with humans can be fatal for the baboons. Many individuals in this group have lost their hands from traps. Some got shot and lost a leg. The alpha male who was judged to be too aggressive and dangerous has already been condemned to death.

This is the fate of just one group of monkeys.
Imagine how other animals are feeling worldwide.

It is not only animals who have consciousness and feelings. Other forms of life, be they trees, flowers, or fungi, also have an ability to communicate.

Early on in the year 2022, one piece of scientific news that was shared widely on the internet was the decoding of the electric current rhymths that the fungi hyphae or thread network was sending to one another. It was found to be a pattern of a language. There was a kind of sentence structure not too different from human languages. At this preliminary stage, scientists were able to identify about 50 words.

The discovery that the world of fungi and plants talk was not new. Suzanne Simard of the University of British Columbia discovered in 1997 a fungi thread network connected to the tree roots of the entire forest. The science journal *Nature* who published the article called it the 'wood wide web', comparing it to the human 'World Wide Web'.

We have long known that trees have a close relationship with fungi. We call it mychorrhiza, literally root fungi. The fungi threads grow into the plant roots. They decompose organic matter in the soil into soluble nutrients and send it to the plants, in exchange for the sugar that plants get from photosynthesis.

In the earth beneath just one of our feet, there are hundreds of kilometres of fungi threads. We know how important these are for decomposing and recycling nutrients in a forest. It is so important we could actually say the mighty forest visible to us above ground is just one half of the forest community, the other half is underground.

That, we knew. What we did not know was that fungi also plays another major role.

The interwoven fungi threads interconnect the tree roots of the whole forest together. It creates a network that coordinates the working of the entire forest as a super-organism.

This Wood Wide Web network is far more complex than our world wide web technology. It sends both information and chemicals, ranging from the basic nutrients such as carbon, nitrogen, phosphorus, water, to hormones, genetic materials, and defence signals.

In this way, trees in a forest community can communicate and take care of one another through the underground network of fungi threads.

This system allows trees to send news. If there is an encroaching danger, trees can make necessary preparations in advance. They could, for example, produce a chemical compound toxic to animals who want to feed on them. They could even send defensive substance to one another. It allows stronger trees to take care of weaker ones when necessary. A mother tree could take care of her children growing further away. Some tree species have a special relationship with another species because they have different times for optimum food production. Take the birch and Douglas Fir, for instance. In the summer the birch produces more food, which can be shared with the Douglas Fir, but in the fall when the birch sheds its leaves, the fir remains evergreen and so could send food over.

The big, old trees are the most important. Suzanne calls them the Mother Trees. They have the highest capacity to access and accumulate resources, so they can share more with the others. One Mother Tree can connect to hundreds of trees in a forest. Perhaps the most amazing finding so far is that when a Mother Tree is dying, she starts to transfer both her resources and knowledge to her children, sending them both chemical compounds and other kinds of signals.

Suzanne Simard's research pioneers a new frontier in natural science, which changes our perspective on plants and fungi in the plant community.

Today she has founded a huge, long-term research project called 'The Mother Tree Project'. It is 100-years long, aiming to study all dimensions of connection and the mechanisms of the wood wide web, including the intricate relationship among the forest biodiversity in detail. This will enhance our understanding of how to handle climate change. It is a gigantic, ambitious project that draws in collaboration from various fields of ecology, as well as young volunteers and local tribes of forest people.

In her book *Finding the Mother Tree: Discovering the Wisdom of the Forest*, Suzanne Simard never says outright if she has ever communicated with trees directly without the help of scientific apparatuses, but if we read between the lines there is a slight suggestion that she may have had such experiences. Her mission, however, is to use the scientific process to provide proof that can persuade government policy to cease the practice of clear-cutting forests for timber.

Monica Gagliano of the University of Southern Cross, Australia, is another frontier scientist who is pioneering an understanding of plant consciousness. She is a generation after Simard, and she is a very courageous woman. She says it outright in her book *Thus Spoke the Plants: A Remarkable Journey of Groundbreaking Scientific Discoveries and Personal Encounters with Plants* that it is co-written with plants. They told her what messages they wanted to get across and helped her design the experiments. For example, proving that plants can 'hear' was simply done by blocking seedlings from physical contact with moisture, while having a pipe of running water along one side of the wall. The sound of the running water was the only stimulant the plants could sense, and their roots grew in that direction.

Monica pioneers a new frontier of research known as 'Plant Bioacoustics' or how plants use sounds. She has shown that plants can create sound waves or what the traditional Plant Medicine people call the 'song' of each plant species. The first time she encountered a plant song was through a spiritual experience under the guidance of a South American Shaman. To prepare to enter the state where she was ready to receive the experience she fasted and meditated. The song is at the end of the frequency that human ears are capable of hearing, so normally we do not detect it. Scientific apparatus, however, can pick it up as a clicking rhythm. We still do not know how plants make the sound waves. Research has only just begun.

It is interesting that Monica's experiments to prove plant consciousness are classic textbook scientific experiments in a laboratory with perfectly controlled variables, but the original idea came from an intuition that scientific circles tend to reject.

Her famous piece of research is recounted at the beginning of the book. Interested readers can listen to it on the YouTube channel called *Bioneers*. Search for "Plant Intelligence and the Importance of Imagination in Science". It is an experiment with a humble bean plant, inspired by Ivan Pavlov's experiment of training of dogs to recognize the sound of bell calling them to dinner. Dogs normally dribble when they get food, and have no response to the sound of a bell ringing. However, when the bell is regularly rung at the feeding time, dogs would associate the sound of bell ringing with getting fed. Trained dogs would salivate at the sound of the bell even when there was no food in front of them.

It was a simple experiment to show that dogs have imagination. They detect signals around them and interpret their meanings. The sound of a bell ringing connects their thoughts to things that are not there. Food is just an idea, an expectation. It is imagination.

For the beans, their food is the blue light used for photosynthesis. Monica uses a small fan in place of the bell in the dog experiment. The way the bean plants responded to the blue light was to lean their shoots towards the light source, but they did not have any reaction to a light breeze. However, when Monica tried turning on the fans regularly at the same time as turning on the light, she found that when she only turned on the fan, the beans would start leaning in that direction despite there being no light.

The little bean plants associated the breeze from the fan with the source of their food. They have expectations just as dogs do. Food or light was just "a thought". It was not something that existed in front of them. Plants, therefore, also have imagination.

This research shakes up present-day human perceptions of plants. We may not yet understand all the processes of plant life, but we have to admit that organisms do not need to have brains and nervous system like vertebrate animals in order to have responses similar to thoughts.

Monica Gagliano sees imagination as a bridge that connects the thinking brain to the feeling heart. It is a life blessing – for all lives. Not all dogs and bean plants show equal reactions. There is a degree of response and variables among different individuals, and from day to day. That implies there is an assessment of need within each individual. It reflects a value system and a decision-making process among different living beings.

During the first ten years when she was conducting these researches, Monica was ridiculed by many scientific colleagues in the university. But no matter how much they wanted to put her down, to laugh at a tree-hugger like her, they could not find a flaw in her experiments and deductions.

Ten years ago, the kind of things Monica was doing seemed to be laughably silly in the eyes of modern society. However, when anthropologists talk to medicine people in indigenous tribes across the world, they found that the knowledge of plants' medicinal properties did not come from random trial and error as we in modern society have assumed. Rather, it came from messages sent by the plants themselves.

Plants, especially trees, seem to have special roles in the world community other than the physical role where they act as a bridge between different states, like converting sun energy into storable chemical energy, or the role of maintaining the earth's atmosphere by storing carbon and releasing oxygen. While they join the earth to the sky, they seem to be keepers of certain knowledge, since they have never been disconnected from the original source of life.

The Thai author, Pojana Chantarasanti, wrote in his book *Dae Chai Noom Lae Ying Sow* (To Young Men and Women):

> "I believe that before the time of language, ancient humans communicated by sending and receiving thoughts directly. These days we call it 'telepathy', which is a lost art. Therefore, human communication then was probably more complete, less distorted. Because of this, it is possible that communication was not limited to that from human and human, but included animals, plants, rocks, minerals and elements in nature too. Since communication was not dependent on voice, words, or language, but used life energy wavelengths directly, it allows humans to communicate fully with all things in nature."

Pojana sees stories where humans talk with animals as remnant traces of this skill in our cultures.

We cannot deny that the invention of elaborate verbal languages to communicate among ourselves is a remarkable ability of our species. Today we have about 6,500 languages that we use to converse with one another. They open a huge gateway to the development of complex human civilizations. Language is a tool we use to transfer accumulated knowledge, create great stories, religions, philosophies; it enables us to gather the masses and become a society that shares similar beliefs. Then on the other side of the coin, verbal language has made us forget the universal language that other lives on earth use to communicate with each other.

The modern society we have grown up in negates telepathy. Claims of its use is seen as a con scheme to trick gullible fools, or it is thought to be an unusual special gift of only a few people. But telepathy is actually a kind of sense that we all have, and probably needed in our co-evolution with other species. We've just forgotten it.

The ability, however, is still ingrained within everyone of us. We can wake it up and train it.

Today there are many people who make a living as animal communicators, and there are courses on offer all over the world, including via on-line learning. The quality may vary, as do other abilities, but it should be noted that it is an experience a lot of people have. They share their experiences, a common pattern emerges, and can develop in teaching courses.

It may seem impossibly complex, but Anna Breytenbach explains the natural simplicity of interspecies-communication as such:

> "It's a simple matter of quieting the mind and intending to connect. The animals pick that up right away, very easily. Then I send either a mental image, or a thought, or an emotion… whatever comes naturally. There's no effort required on the sending side of things. Transference happens at a quantum level, in the universal language of pure energy.
>
> Animals simply show their truths energetically, and that incoming message on my side gets drawn up from the unconscious, intuitive reception to my conscious mind – at which point my brain will attach a mental image, word, sensation or emotion to it. That's already the first layer of "interpretation", and some things can get lost in "translation."

There are, therefore, two parts that need training: the sending out of a message, and the receiving of a message.

Sending out a message may be easy, but it needs to be clearly intended. We emit energy all the time even when we are idle. It is important that our projection is not intense, but it is clear. Think of a time when we are sensing energy from other people. What makes you feel that a person is somewhat unsafe and it is better to keep a good distance; yet, another person seems relaxed and approachable?

That's how it is with intention. If you come on too strong, too directed and sharp, it is scary, like being targeted by a hunter. Everyone wants to hide away. Instead, we need to be still and relaxed, sending out an intention in a light, gentle manner, which is yet clear and powerful.

Put aside doubts and worries. Clear away busy thoughts and emotions. Those have nothing to do with you right now. Then stand up erect, back straight and feet grounded, as if you have a very deep root. The top of your head is held up and connected to the sky. Breathe in deeply to clear the body, like opening windows to let in fresh air, expelling stale air, dust, and any negativity down to the earth to process them, so they become fertilizers to the soil. Then open up all the senses to receive the world. Finally, zip open your heart, and invite an animal, plant, or any other being you wish to communicate with to connect with you.

You may then feel pulled towards a certain direction. Trust that feeling, and follow it.

When you find the being that you are connected to, try to open up a conversation. Perhaps start with introducing yourself.

To receive a message, it is even more important to be still and empty. It is far too easy to interpret a message with a projection of your personal experience. It is actually not that different from deep listening to our fellow human beings in the way we need to listen to the subtle energy of the person we are talking to, not just what she/he says verbally.

I learn Kungfu at Thai-Shaolin Kungfu School. Master Zhu, whom we call *Sifu*, has a way to teach us to perceive intentions. With me, Sifu would say things in Chinese that I'm not familiar with (as it is, I only know how to count 1-10 in Mandarin). If I react to a word I don't

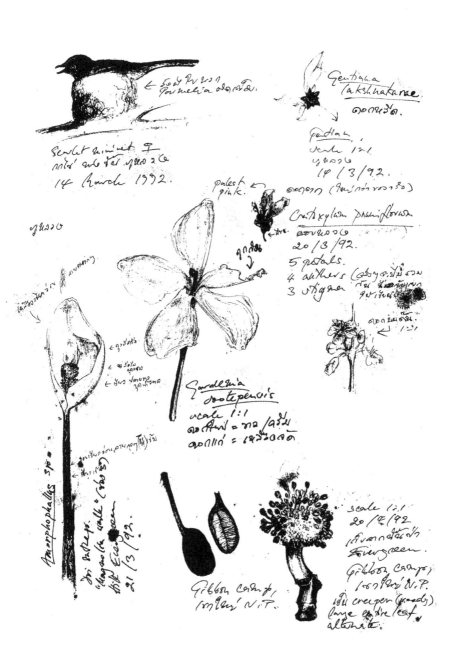

Chapter 6 – Communicating across species

understand, for instance, by stopping in my tracks and turning to look at Sifu, I would fail the test.

What I needed to learn was to listen to the intention behind the word I did not understand. The simplest one was to hear a command of stop or continue. Whatever word he used, the tone would reveal different intentions.

Sending out messages is therefore much easier than receiving. To receive a message and interpret it, we really need to be still and absolutely present in the moment. The more still and empty we are, the clearer the ability to receive.

Animals are so much better than us at this. They tend to be more present in the moment, so they may send and receive subtle wavelengths in the zone of Grace or energetic field at the quantum level more readily than modern humans.

When I saw the documentary *The Animal Communicator* featuring Anna Breytenbach, I had an urge to try communicating with my dearest dog Mie Khow. Mie Khow was a huge Labrador with excessive energy, wanting to play and show his affection all the time. The problem was he liked to leap up and hug us, throwing his entire weight upon us, which if we were not prepared, could easily knock us over.

That night I had a proper talk with Mie Khow before going to bed. I told him how difficult it was for me to bear his weight. I could fall and get hurt. I then offered him an alternative action to show his affection by visualizing him rubbing himself at my side instead.

The next morning, I came downstair from my bedroom. Mie Khow ran to me happily as he always did. When he reached me, he was about to leap, but then he remembered, stopped suddenly in his tracks, and changed to rubbing himself against me. He was like that the whole day. By the following day, rubbing my side to say hello had become his new behaviour.

I was so proud of Mie Khow.

I, on the other hand, don't know how well I understood his needs. Often I felt we understood each other well, but it was just a feeling. I never received a clear visual like he got from me.

At least, Mie Khow and I were close. It's a lot more difficult with an animal who may want to communicate with me but is not my personal friend.

Like my encounter with little baby Banded Krait.

It was in Chiang Dao, Northern Thailand. At the time I had just built a house in the middle of the paddy fields. Like a typical old-fashioned Thai of my grandmother generation, I have a respect for the spirits of a place. I let them know of people coming and going. Although I do not usually light incense ceremoniously, I tell them in my thoughts.

That day I had a person staying in the downstair bedroom, and I forgot to tell the spirits of the place. When she packed up to leave, she screamed.

A little baby Banded Krait was coiled beside her luggage.

I have no idea what I was thinking – more likely I wasn't thinking at all – but instead of scooping up the little snake with a broom and a long-handled dust pan to put it back in the wild, I grabbed her case and led her by the hand to pay respects to the spirit of the place at the spirit house before driving her to the bus station, leaving the snake where it was. I asked the spirit to take care of all the sentient beings in the place, but let each one of us be. The area around my house is my place. Please accept each other's territories.

I didn't go home right away after dropping my house guest off at the bus station. Instead I went for a chat with my neighbour, telling her about the Banded Krait. As I was telling the story, it suddenly occurred to me what an idiot I had been for not handling the snake right away. How would I know now if the snake had left the house. It could be hiding in some corner or other. This was totally insane.

It was dark when I got home. As I walked from the garage to the house, I was pondering if I should leave the door of the downstairs bedroom open that night, so the snake could leave. When I got to the house, however, what I saw was the baby snake resting in exactly the same place I had left it. When it saw me, it raised its head slightly to look at me as if to say, "Look lady, take note, I am leaving your house", and it slithered away.

It was waiting for me for hours, just so that I saw it depart.

I felt so grateful, thanking both the snake and the spirits of the place. I felt a bit bad that it had had to wait for me so long. Had my receptivity not been so blunt, and I could pick up a remote message like picking up a phone, the little snake would not have had to wait around for hours.

Sometimes I feel all beings in nature are infinitely patient with us.

When I thought back about this story ten years later, I was amazed by such a strange incident.

The woman who stayed at the house turned out to be someone who tried to cheat me a few years later. It was the only time a highly poisonous snake appeared at home, coiling itself beside her luggage, and behaving in the oddest manner by waiting hours for me to return home to see it leave the house. I could not help but wonder a little if it was trying to tell me something. Perhaps it was acting as a messenger to greet and communicate with me in a similar way to the seal of the Salish Sea.

When such thoughts emerged, I would check myself and tell myself to stop. I was afraid of being delusional, preferring to choose logic and reasons.

Nonetheless, I believe that inter-species conversation is a trainable skill. I once took a course taught by Judy McAllister of the Findhorn Foundation when she visited Thailand in 2017. The process she taught was not so different from what Anna Breytenbach said. She just broke it down into a detailed process and led us through in small steps, such as grounding and setting up an energetic boundary where communication would take place. Doubts, worries, rambling thoughts are put down outside the circle. Hearts are open and connected.

Judy is a wonderful teacher. There is a certain energy about her that allows us to feel her authenticity. She is down to earth, very articulate, straightforward and very clear. She never beats about the bush or try to be diplomatic. Everyone can accept her frankness, because it comes from kindness. She speaks to our hearts and has such faith in us. She knew right away that I could sense things but was not ready to accept them. However, the skill Judy taught requires regular practice, and I still have to develop it. It is not a tangible technique that one can teach like knitting. The teacher can only guide us, the same way as we have to practice vipassana or other meditations.

There are times though that I received messages clearly. It is the story of the next chapter.

Chapter 7
Co-create together

"Well now that we have seen each other," said the unicorn, "if you'll believe in me, I'll believe in you. That's a great bargain."

~ *Through the Looking-Glass*, Lewis Carroll

In the story of Super Wolf No.21 in chapter 5, I mentioned the degraded condition of Yellowstone National Park at the time he was born, but I haven't said what it was like at the time of his death. 70 years before the parents of Twenty-One were brought to Yellowstone, humans had killed all the wolves and wiped them off the land. The consequences were devastating. The elk population had increased unchecked, grazing all the vegetation till it was almost barren. Without plant cover, the soil got eroded. Sediments filled the river till it became shallow and lost its course. When it rained, the water simply ran off all over the place. The animals that used to live in the old habitats disappeared.

Then conservationists brought back 14 grey wolves in 1995 and released them into the park. The state of the habitats has changed rapidly ever since.

Of course, the wolves ate the elks, but the reduced number of elks was not the biggest issue. George Monbiot, a noted environmental journalist, related in a TED talk that became a video clip "How Wolves Change Rivers" on a YouTube channel, Sustainable Human, that the biggest impact was that the wolves caused the elks to change their behaviour. Elks were no longer the biggest rulers of the land. They could no longer graze plants at leisure anywhere. They needed to hide and avoid places where they could easily be trapped and hunted down, particularly around the valleys and gorges. These areas then started to regenerate immediately. In some places tree saplings shot up five times in height within just six years. The valley sides that were bare, devoid of vegetation, quickly changed into forests of aspen, willow, and cotton wood.

With the recovery of the trees, birds also returned. The number of songbirds and migratory birds increased manyfold. Beavers were also back, since they chew up trees. As with wolves, beavers are ecosystem engineers, creating habitats for other lives. The weirs they build on the rivers are not the same as rigid manmade dams. Not only do they not obstruct the lives of other animals, they also provide micro habitats for otters, muskrats, ducks, fish, reptiles, and amphibians.

Wolves also killed cayotes, resulting in an increased number of rabbits and mice, which meant an increase in medium-size hunters like hawks, weasels, foxes, and badgers. Ravens and bald eagles came down to eat carrion that the wolves had left. Bears too fed on carrion, and their numbers went up, partly also because there were now more berries growing on the regenerated shrubs. Like wolves, bears also killed some deer. calves

The most remarkable thing, however, was the impact wolves had on the behaviour of the rivers. From running off and meandering widely all over the place, they began to take a course, and were eroding less. The channels narrowed down, creating more pools and riffles, all of which are great habitats for all sorts of wildlife.

The rivers changed in response to the wolves, because regenerating forests held up the river banks, making them more stable. And because deer were driven away in some areas, and vegetation on the valley sides recovered and protected the soil, there was less erosion, hence less sediments being washed down.

So wolves are not just killers. They also give life, many more lives than they eat. It works through an intricate, complex cascading food web, where wolves are the top predators.

 All of us, all lives, create an impact that proceeds in a domino fashion through the system. As the saying from Chaos Theory goes, "a flutter of butterfly's wing can ultimately cause a typhoon half way around the world". The atmosphere and the water we depend on remain in a state conducive to life through interactions among all beings and things that at times counter balance one another, or support one another. All of our lives, every species, are like different organs of the living planet Earth. It is like a super-organism.

If the flap of a butterfly wing can cause impacts, imagine the activities of *Homo sapiens* over the past 140 years since we have dug up fossils to burn for fuel, accelerate global warming and cause climate change. We have hunted out and exterminated numerous fellow species inhabitanting the planet. Even animals with a seemingly overwhelming population, like the Passenger Pigeon in North America, which was estimated to be as many as 3-5 billion in number, making up about 30-40% of bird population in 19th-century United States. Or, in Thailand, the case of Schomburgk's Deer in the Chao Phraya river floodplain. This was the deer with the most elaborate antlers in the world, and was found only in Thailand before they were hunted to extinction. Or consider the impacts of manufacturing nitrogen-based fertilizers that extracts nitrogen from the air using enormous amounts of energy, then throws it onto the soil to boost food plant yeild, killing lives in the soil in the process. It's then washed down into the rivers and the sea, killing off aquatic life. There's also the production of new materials, alien to natural ecosystems like plastic that earth microbes cannot yet decompose. Not to mention nuclear waste that will continue to emit radiation for millions of years to come.

Humans are challenging the mechanism that has been keeping the earth in balance by behaving like cancerous cells, which the planet will eventually get rid off.

That balance, nonetheless, tends to happens naturally through ecological flow. It is not intended.

But what if we actually set out with a specific intention to co-create something in collaboration with other living beings, tapping into one another's intelligence and particular capacities?

In Africa, humans have a special relationship with Honeyguides, wild birds that nobody raises or trains, but which communicate with humans whenever there is a need to carry out a special mission together, namely to retrieve a beehive. The birds know in which tree hollow bees have built their hive, while the humans have fire and the ability to smoke out the bees from their hive and open up the tree hollow. Humans likes to eat the honey, while the birds like to eat the wax.

Both humans and birds have special sounds they use specifically for communicating with one another, not unlike siblings with a private special language understood only among themselves. It is interesting that the human sounds used to call the birds differ in different places. For example, in Northern Mozambique, the honey-hunting Yao tribe would make a "Brrrr…hm!" call to signal to the bird that they were ready to go and get honey. A Honeyguide would come and lead the way. Whereas the Hadza tribe in Northern Tanzania whistles a particular tune.

Sometime the Greater Honeyguide is the one who initiates the hunt when it finds a bee hive it wants to eat. In such a case, the bird would fly to a human and gives a chattering call "Je-je-je-je", indicated the people should follow.

This is a relationship between two independent and free species who are willing to support one another. It gives a glimpse of a probable way of life that humans may have had with other fellow inhabitants of the planet in an ancient times. Still, this is just a joint activity to get something that already exists. It is not the creation of something new.

However, there are situations in which the relationship between humans and other living beings can lead to co-creating something together.

An example most often cited is the case of the Findhorn community in Scotland. It all began with three people who had lost their jobs in a hotel in the early 1960s, namely Dorothy Maclean, Peter and Eileen Caddy, along with their three children. They could only afford to live in a caravan parked on a barren coastal land by the North Sea. The three adults practiced meditation regularly. When they started to grow vegetables for food on that poor, sandy soil, they received instruction from other beings, whom they called 'angels'. The produce turned out to be beautifully healthy and abundant, be they flowers or fruits and vegetables. The most famous items were the gigantic cabbages that were bigger than any other cabbages in the world, weighing as much as 18 kilograms.

When the news spread, scientists came to inspect the soil and examine the environment. They were baffled. They could not explain the phenomenon of the super-cabbage.

Findhorn started to attract people with an interest in nature and spiritual matters. The community grew into a village. In 1972 it was registered as the Findhorn Foundation, offering various workshops and courses both at the foundation and other places across the world. Today, the Findhorn Foundation is still in operation even though the original three founders have passed away. Those who are interested can check out at www.findhorn.org

The Findhorn residents refer to angels as the norm. Actually, we are probably the only generation of people in the course of human history who negate the existence of spirits, ghosts, fairies, angels and all invisible beings. The best take, at least in Thailand, is adopting an attitude of "Do not believe, but do not show disrespect" to honour the beliefs of previous generations.

Personally, I feel there are such beings co-existing with us on this earth, though I do not know much about them. I did not really understand the business of co-creating with other species either, until it happened to me. It was to be an experience that changed my understanding of the world.

As mentioned in previous chapters, I believe that our ability to communicate with other species is still intact within us. We just need to awaken it, and train the muscle again.

Although I believed this to be so, I had not expected how relatively easy the ability could be recalled.

A few years before the outbreak of Covid-19, my colleagues and I offered short courses on nature connection for the general public. The first day we would focus on refining the basic senses through various exercises, and we would end the day at 'Job's Grove', a small woody patch in the middle of the rice fields that my husband planted in the mid 1990s, not far from the workshop base at our house. The activity we do there is commonly known as 'Meet A Tree' or what Thai nature educators call 'My Dear companion Tree'. There are many variations on the activity, but generally the facilitator would blindfold each participant and lead him/her to a tree that the facilitator chooses, leaving him/her there to get to know the tree through all the senses except sight. After a short while, the facilitator would then bring the participants back to the starting point, untie the blindfolds, and let them return to their trees based on the memories of their senses. This could be the texture of the trunk, sizes and shapes, smell, temperature, and a few people would even rely on intuitive senses of some kind. Whatever sense they used, everyone would always find his/her tree.

At first, I was not quite sure if I was imagining it, but it seemed to be an activity that the trees in this grove liked as much as the workshop participants. I felt the trees told me they wanted to know people and play the role of nature's ambassador. Then one day before a workshop, I woke up early at dawn, opened the door and stepped out onto the front balcony, from where I had a clear view of Job's Grove.

The air was fresh and cool. The sacred mountain of Chiang Dao stood before me, majestic and powerful. I was in a light and empty state of mind, ready to take on the new day. Suddenly, I was aware of a mass of thoughts shooting out of Job's Grove down into the top of my head, like an airdrop app with a file that downloaded into a thought in my brain. It suggested a change in the process of meeting a tree. The trees wanted to take part in the activity: they wanted to be the ones who choose their human friends.

I would like to make a special note here. Although I tend to describe the act of receiving messages as 'downloading', which may make it sound cold and mechanical, it is not really like that. It happens when we have a line of friendly connection. I would also like to add that in the act of communication, there is no power play where one side is of a higher status than the other and gets to control the relationship. We cannot force other beings to talk to us if they do not want to. We need to ask for permission. When a being initiates an approach, it too has to wait for our reception. It is a relationship based on mutual respect. We are equal in our rights to be here. Every time a fellow planetary inhabitant shows a wish to talk to me, I am touched and feel very grateful.

The problem is once I received a message in the form of a thought from the tree grove, a part of me naturally doubted if it really came from the trees or if it was just my imagination. Then again, it was totally unlike me to come up with such idea. In a situation where it was my responsibility and I was accountable for the outcome, I wanted to have a certain control. So, I bargained to have a Plan B, and we had a deal.

When we arrived at Job's Grove, participants were paired up. One would close his/her eyes, while the other would act as a guide. Instead of the facilitator, i.e. me, being the one who choose a tree for each guide to take his/her partner to, I asked the guides to stand grounded, rooted to the earth, head to the sky, opening up all their senses. When ready, the guides then opened wide his/her heart, while asking internally which tree here in this grove would want to meet my friend here, who is closing his/her eyes? The guides were asked to put all doubts aside for the time being, and whatever feeling came up, they should take on the cue and lead the friend to that tree. Plan B was if two guides happened to choose the same tree, the one who arrived later would simply scan his/her feelings again to find a new tree.

We have run the activity many times since, but hardly anyone has ever gone for the same tree even though it is only a small grove, with the number of trees almost matching the number of human participants.

Many participants spoke of a very clear force of attraction that pulled them towards the trees. Very often when they opened their eyes, they would see one tree clearly in focus, while others melted away in the background like the effect in portrait photography. Some felt a tinkling vibration that pointed to a certain direction. Some set an intention for one tree, but when they put the question out there, their attention was shifted to another. One person told of a spotlight shining on another tree. Each tree also seemed to match the person who was led blindfolded to it. For example, it might have a dark, almost black bark, just how she liked it. In another case the tree was bearing fruits, just as he was imagining, or the tree had a texture that felt comforting. One person related how she was afraid of insects that might bite or sting her, but suddenly was awash with a reassurance that the tree would take good care of her, and she immediately felt safe.

Once, a guide took a participant who was familiar with the trees in Job's Grove to a tree to which she felt a strong attraction. She did not know that her partner had had a past experience with that particular tree. It was abundantly clear that the tree chose its old friend. What was more, this old friend was a mathematical nerd well trained in the scientific process. Every time he had an experience that seemed 'supernatural', he

Chapter 7 – Co-create together

would always find a sensible explanation to counter it. I simply advised him to keep notes, building up his data for statistical evaluation.

This time he made an experiment, and set out to limit his own sensing of the tree. He did not put his arms around its trunk to gauge its dimension, nor did he feel around to sense its shape and texture. He simply placed his two hands on the tree, and stayed still.

When he was brought back to the base and opened his eyes, he turned round and knew immediately that the tree that chose him was his old friend. There was a certain feel that brought the tree to his visual foreground. It was crystal clear, no doubt whatsoever.

When we returned from Job's Grove, no one doubted any more that trees had consciousness.

But the biggest lesson learned was my own. I was one of many Thai citizens who had actively campaigned for democracy in our human society, yet I had only just begun to be aware of how I had overlooked the participatory process for other species stake holders. It was only because they looked so different from us, so much that I could not see their capabilities.

I have just begun to learn how we should try to listen more to trees and other fellow beings. I need to learn to trust their wisdom, just as I listen to the voices of people in human society.

The quality of the work we do is taken up to another level when we listen and co-create with other species, taking on a dimension we could never achieve on our own. It expands the boundary of possibilities in a way we could not imagine.

Chapter 8

Blend the outer and the inner worlds

"Kungfu is balance. Balance is Kungfu"
~ Qiguo Zhu, Thai Shaolin School

The midday sun in an open savanna forest during the hot, dry season in Huai Kha Khaeng Wildlife Sanctuary in Western Thailand is no joke. It is fierce, bright and scorching. I tried to stand still, raising my face and opening up to the glaring sun, trying to imagine and pretending to be a tree.

After just 10 minutes I had to retreat for a cover under the shade of a tree and gulped down some water.

I get it. Trees are not like us. They receive energy directly from the sun, making their own food. An animal like me cannot really imagine what it's like. But the sun is not just the source of energy and temperature that living beings need, it is also heat that sucks up water from our bodies. This is a problem trees have to deal with. The biggest challenge, however, is whenever a problem confronts them, they cannot run away from it like we animals do. They need to rely entirely on their own capacity to deal with the issue, face on.

I was doing field research on forest fire ecology at the time. It aroused a sense of awe in me and a deep respect for trees. These beings had to deal with fire hotter than 700 degree Celsius. How did they cope with the heat? More than that, how do their offspring, the baby seedlings and teenage saplings, cope with it and gather enough strength to grow into big trees that can take on the world. Trees never escape problems.

Looking at the world from the perspectives of other species and how they meet challenges has since become an approach I often use in my scientific communication with the public to instigate fascination. It invites appreciation of how brilliant other species are, often a brilliance so very different from our own.

Nonetheless, while I thought I was delving deep into my heart to appreciate and understand, as I racked my brain in search for new angles of looking at challenges, my work tended to present a narrative based on science.

This book is totally different from anything I've written before. In the past, I focused on telling ecological stories, such as the amazing adaptations of various lives on earth, inviting readers to see the world from their perspectives. I made special efforts to empower young people to be able to read nature and what's going on around them, so they could access information themselves and build up their own knowledge of the local environment. I initiated citizen science projects, way before the term was coiled, together with handbooks for 'environmental detectives'. These ranged from *Stream Detectives* that take people to explore the aquatic life in streams and rivers, and begin to understand what's going on there. Is the stream healthy or does it have a problem? I then moved on to *Seashore Detectives*, investigating the lives of the mudflats, sandy beaches, rocky shores, and the tidal zone, followed by *Air Detectives* that assesses the quality of the air we breathe from the presence of lichens in a city.

It is only in the past 10 years that I have promoted an agenda of nature connection to revive human's relationship with nature, while still staying within the boundary of what science has proven.

In the eyes of people who do not know me well, I am a person who only sees the world through scientific processes. Scientists themselves tend to get labelled as lacking in spiritual sensitivity.

In a society that splits knowledge into categories of disciplines, and even classifies people into different levels of intelligence based on the disciplines they're linked with, we tend to put each other into boxes with attached labels. Some may make generalizations and ridicule others to elevate their own status.

When I was a kid, Thai society saw children who were good at science as the brightest, followed by social science and literature. The least intelligent were the artists and the athletes. We all grew up with complexes. To counter the labels, the arty people looked down on the science people as square-headed, with no creativity, no depth of feelings and spiritually shallow.

Science people took on such prejudices. There are some medical doctors who, having discovered a sense of harmony in the arts, go about giving talks on how to appreciate beauty, and acting like the most evolved humans on the self-development scale. They are even higher than their fellow A-grade students who are already seen as the top-notches of Thai society.

I face this kind of disdain all the time. Sometime I find it funny, other times I get annoyed. The worst thing is I have developed a reverse prejudice. I don't want to befriend them, and so we have a wall between us.

Once my younger brother and I went on a trip to a forest with a bunch of environmental educators who used various approaches. We were in the back of a pick-up truck, driving through a green tunnel on a tree-lined dirt road. My brother and I were happy to be in the forest. We were excited and joyful, pointing out birds and flowers to one another

Suddenly there was a loud whisper, jeering at us with soft laughter and calling us "there goes the *jit song ok nok* people", meaning people who let their minds drift outside of themselves.[1]

The speakers were deep ecologists, who emphasized fasting and meditation in the wilderness. This particular group – and I stress this particular group, not the whole or even the majority of deep ecology movement – tended not to be very interested in the living things around them.

When standing in a stream, this particular type of deep ecologist would meditate, delving deep into the sound of the flowing water and their inner spiritual world, while stacking up stones from the stream bed into a pile resembling a shrine, as is often seen in the Himalayan region.

They never noticed the little aquatic insects who were living on those rocks, wriggling for life on the pile of carefully stacked stones. They never understood the meaning of air bubbles breaking out when water splashes onto the rocky streambed and how important it is for aquatic life. Rocks and stones on riffles are the lungs of a stream. Remove lots of them, and the amount of oxygen dissolved in the stream water will decrease. It impacts the animals who need water with a high oxygen content. Many more cannot lay their eggs.

---

1 It is a saying used in Buddhist meditation practice, referring to an act of letting the mind drifts toward outside stimulants and react to sensations created, while forgetting to pay attention to what's happening to the mind and body at the present moment.

Areas where these deep ecologists camp out are often full of stone stacks. It pains me to see the empty houses of net-spinning caddisflies dried out on these stones. This aquatic insect weaves a net which looks rather like a soccer goal cage on a rock to catch organic debris that flows downstream for food. Sometimes aquatic insects cannot get back into the water, and their dried-up bodies remain stuck on a stone stack. I almost always deconstruct these stone piles whenever I come across them in a stream.

Conservationists in the Mediterranean campaign against this practice too. Summer sun in the dry terrain is incredibly strong, so rocks are important hideout places for many animals. It is particularly crucial for the skinks who need to keep their skin moist. Their population has plummeted when hikers brought the practice of stacking stones back from the Himalayas. It may be considered a spiritual practice, although most of the time people in the Himalayas do it to make a trail mark.

Observing the outer world of lives around us is therefore just as important as observing the inner world of the spiritual self. It is the practice of paying attention to others and helps us to not see ourselves as the centre of the universe.

Another so called spiritual activity in Thai culture is that of releasing captured animals back into the wild for merit-making. But what good is that if the deed causes harm to other living beings? Why would we want to release alien African catfish with big wide mouths and let them gobble up all the local wild fishes in the stream? There is also a puzzling trend of building weirs across streams to slow down water flow and hold back sediments, in the belief that this is good for the environment by supposedly keeping soil in the surrounding area moist. It has no scientific basis, yet the practice is immensely popular in modern Thai society, and is often sponsored by big corporations as well as government agencies. This so called 'Do Good Deed' programme is, in actual fact, an act of ecosystem destruction, a sabotage of animal homes. It has caused the extinction of certain dragonflies and hill stream fish, and perhaps many more that we do not know about.

Good intentions alone are not enough to create good outcomes. We need to understand the needs of other species. We need to seek an understanding of the working of natural forces that drive and govern a local landscape.

It is pointless to keep competing as which thing is better than another. At this critical time, we need to stop swinging between extremes and find a balance.

On the wall of the Thai Shaolin Kungfu School is written:

"Kungfu is balance, balance is Kungfu.

Find the center of your body"

It's a core message with more profundity than the mere practice of standing stable on one leg like a crane.

When I first started learning kungfu, there were some seniors (who were younger than me) ready to test for a new level, from yellow belt to green. One was a girl, who was somewhat chubby and moved in a simple manner, that was hardly exciting to watch. She moved along with Master Zhu's commands, passing the test easily. The other was a strong young man with the manner of an actor in a Kungfu movie. He did not pass the test.

My perplexed expression must have been clear, for Master Zhu quickly explained to the whole class that at this level, he was looking for a balance between your inner and outer states. They needed to match. In that state of being, everyone would look beautiful in his or her own way.

Although the girl who passed the test was nothing like Michelle Yeoh in her martial art movies, she was completely relaxed and comfortable in her own skin. The flow of her movement matched the relaxed state she was in. In comparison, the young man was nervous. He would not look Master Zhu in the eyes, and was not aware of things going on in his surroundings.

Whoa! I got it.

Never had I had so much fun with any exam before, ever.

The equal states of the outer and inner being is a balance. It is what the Chinese calls *Ping Heng*. It is Kungfu.

Remember a moment when we felt as one with the world around us, when the boundary between our inner self and the outer world melts away. The outer and inner beings blend together as one. We become nature.

In the first chapter I may have stressed that scientific knowledge is not sufficient to lend us wings to get pass the crisis of nature destruction. Science alone cannot enable us to co-exist with other beings who share this planet with us. Still, the sharpness of the analytical mind used in scientific thinking is a powerful tool not to be brushed off lightly. A good scientist is well aware of the limitations that his knowledge can access. And an intelligent human would not negate all the dimensions of his or her capacity.

It is up to us whether we allow our scientific knowledge or learned information to make us become a complacent know-it-all, who can no longer get enthusiastic with the things we encounter, or whether we allow ourselves to have the capacity to be fascinated with our natural surroundings at another level.

I call the latter ability the 'beginner's mind'.

It's that freshness of amazement with the thing we discover for the first time. How would it be if we could maintain that state of mind.

From my personal experience, I've found that a vaccine against apathy lies in contemplation. To stop and contemplate a phenomenon we are so used to is a very powerful action.

For instance, when we watch a sunrise or sunset, our perceived experience tells us that we are standing still on planet Earth with a round sun orbiting across the sky over our head from one horizon to the other. But next time when you watch the sunset, try thinking of the situation we know to be true, that we actually stand on a round earth, which is rotating to our back, away from the sun, creating a visual of the sun setting over the horizon. We are not so different from the illustrations in the book *The Little Prince*.

Most of the information we receive is second-hand knowledge from schools and books. Examples are plant photosynthesis; or the growth of life from fertilization through cell divisions, the development of eyes, heart, and other organs, all happening in the mother's womb, and emerging as us; or the co-evolution between plants and animals until they are adapted to one another and become a perfect fit in physical forms as well as behaviour. A butterfly has a mouthpart like a long hose pipe called a proboscis, that it coils up under its chin. At feeding, the proboscis is uncoiled and probes deep into the long, narrow corolla tube of the *Ixora* flower to get to the nectar at the very bottom, its face touching the front of flower and pollinating it.

We may get excited with some piece of knowledge the first time we read about it, and there's a sense of discovery, but there are also a lot of topics we learned by rote in a traditional classroom, and never felt a feeling of awe even though it might be absolutely fascinating when you really think about it.

Take the capacity of plants, for instance. They convert energy from the sun into storable chemical form, and pass it on to other lives on earth. They are the real alchemists. We may have known about this from our elementary school teacher. It is not something we have discovered ourselves, but we can witness the phenomenon. As kids, my classmates and I carried out a simple experiment of placing half a coconut shell on a grass lawn, until the grass underneath went yellow and almost died. Later in life we garden. We observe patterns of leaf growth in a forest. We become aware that photosynthesis is the most magical process.

Just starting to write about plants leads to the contemplation of further wonders about them. Quiet contemplation not only opens the door to more information, it also helps us to feel the amazing wonder of that information. It suddenly becomes alive.

When contemplation is coupled with close observation, we see new details different from those we have noticed before. A new leaf that unfurls and greets the world is not quite the same as the hundreds of times we have seen it. We feel the freshness. We feel happy that our existing knowledge adds to the joy.

That joy opens a window in our hearts to embrace life force around us, connecting one another.

It is the state of Cat Steven's song, *Morning Has Broken*:

"Morning has broken, like the first morning…
Blackbird has spoken, like the first bird…"

โซนห้วยที่สมบูรณ์ที่สุดที่เคยเห็น
สุดยอด นก Indicator : นกดำน้ำ, Riverchat, Plumbeous Redstart
Forktail, + ชนิดกาเดินก้อนหินกลางน้ำ
สัตว์ benthic abundant ตัวใต้ผิวหนาแน่น (ขนก้อนเผย ๆ กากัน)
ข้าวสาร ตัวใหญ่มากสำหรับน้ำ เมืองไทย
ยุงตัวรี่ แมลงน้ำ เยอะ ปรี๊ด
ตอนเก็บกลับเข้าถักแด้ หรือ ลอกคราบ
เดินตัวเดินวุ่น คลานเลาะเกาะฝืน
เดินก้อนหิน เลื้อย ๆ กะต้วม

"Bungy Jumper"
Caddisfly

Special adaptation
กับน้ำไหลแรง
"เชือก" ที่ตัดออกโยงกับก้อนหิน
เป็นวัสดุจาก ปชิ (รากอ่อน?)
คอยดึงตัว เวลากระแสน้ำโต้
มาทาง กระแสน้ำ
เวลาเข้าดักแด้ จะปิดประตูปอด.

ที่จุดที่ ก. 4/16.
11/3/2000

Cased Caddisfly อยู่ที่นี่
แจคดี มากเป็นสีม่วง ปน
ก้อนพืชๆกก้อน กลับเข้า
ดักแด้ มากพิสดาร = หลบแดด
(ตอนน้ำกระแสแรง)

หัักสิริกุล ขอบสัมพบุรี
ตุลา 1989

Nemouridae?
(ตรวจดูข้อรา
ทรวง ข้อ 2
ต่อ ลันตา ข้อ 1)

unidentified
Plecoptera form.
หัวกะทิชุล
ส่วนแม่กำ Oct 99.

ปลาซิวจาก 1:1
น้ำชีขัด
อ.1ก6
11/3/2000

ก้างลืม ข้าง
ตัวพรา6
ขนาด:

11/3/2000
หัวธาฒิ
อ.พร. ชุมทัรร้อย อ.ปก6.
(อ. บรรจงส์ ส่งว่า
อาจเป็นชนิด เฉพาะถิ่น
Site specific/endemic?)

วาดเสร็จแล้วแต่น
เหงือกดูตัวใหญ่ๆ
แต่ล่านอย
บนหลังจริงๆ.

ขนาด 1:1
(ให้เก็บ
แล้ช่อย
ส่ยผ.)

Chapter 8 – Blend the outer and the inner worlds   129

When we feel that the new day is as the first day of our lives, that the bird singing is as the first bird song we have heard, every tiny part and dimension of nature is always magical. We are in awe.

Quiet contemplation of scientific insights can take us to the fine sensitivity of spiritual being. It is the path of the nerds, and most brilliant biologists I have come across anywhere in the world are people with minds full of wonder with the things they see as if they were seeing them for the first time. That fresh eye gives rise to new questions. The more they observe and contemplate, the more wonder they have, endlessly. The more we know how much we do not know does not matter at all. It is an awareness of ignorance that we can live with happily, and still have fun.

Nature is always fresh and new, even when we believe we could trace the antiquity of a molecule in front of us way back to the moment of the Big Bang.

Simply contemplate and allow your heart to feel.

Epilogue
Towards *Homo gaia*

> "Our planet is alive and aware. By communicating and working with all of nature, humans can find and bring new creative solutions to life."
>
> ~ Dorothy Maclean, one of the founders of
> the Findhorn Foundation

At the beginning of the book I defined *Homo gaia* as "A species of human that renews its membership with the Earth's community, living alongside other beings. It is a human that has evolved beyond the crisis of nature destruction by the *Homo sapiens*."

It is not a definition I have coined myself, but a message from the other species we share the planet with, which many other people have also received on different occasions. I personally got it from a large Pindrow Fir in the Valley of the Flowers in India. How each of us interpret the message into human words may vary in various details.

Judy McAllister, my teacher on interspecies communication from Findhorn, who often talks to big old trees, has noted a message she got from the Atlantic Coastal Rainforest of Brazil in her book *Forest Voices: When Nature Speaks*. Here's an excerpt :

> ".. We call out our welcome. Will you hear? Will you walk silently among us, listening to the sound of the forest, setting aside for a while the sound of your cities. Will you come with your eyes open and see the beauty? Will you come with your hearts open and allow them to break open fully with wonder? Will you come with minds empty of what you want and discover what you need. Will you come and claim your place amongst us? Will you come, that you may know yourself, that we may know each other.
>
> Come. Again and again, the invitation is extended. ...Come. Walk. Watch. Sit. Listen. Feel. Come."

We are in the midst of the Sixth Extinction. This time it is not caused by a meteor crashing into the Earth as happened last time, which caused the extinction of dinosaurs. This time it is caused by human actions.

When the meteor hit the earth, it sent a huge amount of sulphuric dust into the atmosphere and formed a layer that blocked out the sunlight, creating years of long dark winter. As there was not enough sun – the source of energy, coming down to the Earth, the large size of many dinosaurs was no longer an advantage over other animals. The ones that survived were the smaller dinosaurs that evolved into birds. It is the same with humans. Our large brains with sharp, analytical minds that helped us to spread and rule over the world today could very well become our weakness if we are arrogant and use it as a tool to handle every issue, even at a time when we need to use our hearts.

From the perspective of Gaia, we are like mad men who cut off their own limbs.

The Theory of Gaia sees the Earth as a super-organism, operated by the diversity of life, with all kinds of plants, animals, fungi, bacteria and other microbes, interacting with each other in their different roles. At times they support one another, at other times they provide checks and balances. It is often compared to the working of different organs in our body that drive life processes and cycles of matter and energy, maintaining our body in a condition conducive for life.

Biodiversity is therefore related to the efficiency of the working of ecosystem. When some species disappear, the consequences may not be that great. It might be like losing the pinky finger of your left hand. You can still maintain a good quality of life, only maybe your grip is not as stable as before. You can hold fewer chords on a guitar. No big deal. But when a lot of life goes extinct, it is like losing more and more important organs. The spleen is gone, one lung is gone, a piece of your liver is removed. Perhaps your heart is gone, and you have to use an artificial one. You're still alive, but the quality of your life is seriously impaired.

Today, our destruction of nature has caused the disappearance on a terrifying scale of the fellow living beings who share the planet with us, at a scale perhaps 1,000 times the rate of natural extinction. It has left the Earth like a man with two legs amputated.

We are at a ten-way junction. Which road are we going to choose?

Are we going to sit on our wheel chair, knife in hand, ready to cut off the rest of our fingers and hands too? Or perhaps we're going to demand that the surface of the earth be rendered, flat and smooth, convenient for traveling on wheels – essentially adjusting the earth to suit us? Or are we going to design high-quality prosthetic legs, and at the same time taking care of the rest of the body we still have, strengthening our remaining muscles, so we are equipped to live on the earth with its undulating landscapes, rough mountainous terrain, and soft sandy beaches? We would still have a good quality of life, because we are willing to adapt, adopt new ways of thinking, new ways of life, and a new kind of technology that allow us to co-habit with the rest of life on earth.

The ancestors of *Homo gaia* – that is us – are likely to choose a path somewhat similar to the latter one.

At the time of writing, Thailand is facing major obstacles that have been blocking us from moving forward. There is a small group of people with all the power who hoard the majority of the resources, and they are desperately doing everything they can to prevent restructuring, using military coups, an arbitrary justice system, and other power play tactics. They refuse to share, even speeding up their power grabs unchecked. But suppose that we overcome this particular hurdle, and suppose our society gets to the point where we face and accept fully the current planetary crisis, suppose we are ready to find a consensus on our future together, the first things we need to do are

1. Stop initiating and approving projects which destroy nature. We cannot afford to lose anymore of our natural environment. Essentially, stop doing harm.

2. Let nature regenerate everywhere

3. Take on the challenging goal of accelerating towards sustainable development within 10 years. Brainstorm ideas so the transition process than be the least painful, with measures to support everyone so they can adapt and get through.

In the attempt to turn round the dire situation, biodiversity conservation needs to be integrated into all of our actions as the norm. Designating special preservation areas in the form of national parks here and there as we have been doing is important, but it is not enough to care for our fellow living things and create the environmental conditions that can support and sustain our quality of life. Today, these reserved areas are scattered about like islands in a sea of human civilization. Most are not large enough to sustain viable wildlife populations. They tend to be hilly, steep-sloped areas where we don't often choose to cultivate crops and build our cities, so they do not cover all important habitats. Wildlife in these scattered patches cannot travel to connect with each other. We therefore need to have different forms of nature conservation at different levels of preservation. It needs to include agricultural land as well as towns, cities, and peoples' homes, with special protection for the areas and vegetation of the water margins that act as buffer zone between land and aquatic ecosystems. The protected riparian forests and reedbeds also connect different nature reserves, and provide corridors for wildlife to travel to and fro, interact, and have a better chance of maintaining healthy genetic pools.

As we begin to have success in wildlife conservation, we have to be prepared to handle new challenges which are already happening in many places, when the increased wildlife population starts to have conflicts with humans. We would then need more animal communicators like Anna Breytenbach. In the end, unless one side is killed off, all conflicts have to end with negotiations.

In Thailand today there are often conflicts between farmers and wild elephants. Elephants are very intelligent animals, who know how to solve technical problems and know how to make plans, so they are able to counter every move that humans come up with to block them. Whether it be fences or deep trenches, elephants find ways to cross over. They play mind games with humans and can trick them into setting up barricade blockage one way, before quietly taking another route to raid a farmer's crops.

There's a glimmer of hope, however, from a story my sister-in-law told me. Her family has owned a fruit orchard in Chantaburi, Eastern Thailand for generations. Elephant raids in Durian and Mangosteen orchards is a serious problem in the region. They destroy expensive fruit trees that take a long time to grow. Then one year, her neighbour tried talking to the elephants through meditation. He made a plea and offered an alternative solution. He was willing to share the fruits, but he asked that the elephants do so gently. Do not break big branches, do not fell the trees. Otherwise, there won't be any fruits for anyone the following year.

The elephants got the message. They came, they ate some, and did so gently. His orchard has survived and thrived to this day.

With regard to technology and resource management systems, we humans have to change a lot to be like other members of the Gaia Community. We need to use resources efficiently, cycling them without using a lot of energy, and create an environment conducive for living instead of dumping pollutions and waste that cannot be decomposed.

One of the most promising technical solutions that's been developing in these past few decades is an approach known as biomimicry. It is a technology that borrows an idea from other species who have had immense successes in solving certain problems, which have been tested through time over millions of years of evolution. In Japan, a hi-speed Shinkansen train was designed after the beak of a kingfisher to reduce friction, so the train may move fast quietly while saving energy. A building in Zimbabwe mimics the air regulation of an African termite mound, so it can keep cool all year round without the use of any air conditioning. It lowers the cost of maintaining and running the building, which reduces the fixed cost of business operations, and in turn reduces the price of goods and services offered.

The art and science of biomimicry today have gone beyond simply mimicking the physical forms of plants and animals. Researchers from many institutions have been developing solar power that mimics the process of plant photosynthesis. Other ongoing projects include the mimicking of the way coral makes cement. Instead of blasting limestone hills, using immense amounts of heat and releasing tons of carbon in cement manufacturing, carbon could be taken in under a room-temperature environment.

Or, cities, our human habitats, could be managed like the efficient ecological system of the complex tropical rainforest.

How would it be if we could consult our fellow earth dwellers directly on solutions to a range of problems. It might save us a lot of time. Somewhat similar to how plants helped Monica Gagliano with her experiment design in chapter 6.

When *Homo gaia* joins community with other living things on earth, they become people who can access both collective wisdom from human society as well as from other species. This is a hybrid human who has both the ancient skills of our ancestors who lived closely with nature, and the knowledge of modern humans.

However, *Homo gaia* is not a perfect human species without vices, living in a little low-tech palm-leaved roof hut on the forest edge, surrounded by little animal friends like Disney's Snow White. Rather, theirs is a human society with a collective consciousness very different from now. They have a value system and consent to rules of co-existence that respect life and are deeply aware of the importance of ecological health. They have both the technology and the skills to support co-existence with other species.

Homo gaia knows well there is no such thing as super-natural, only very natural. It is a dimension of nature the twentieth-century *Homo sapiens* could not explain. That's all.

Our expanded worldview would elevate our consciousness. Not only would it allow us to have greater empathy for other beings, but it would reconnect our severed relationship with them. It would heal our inadequacies, making us whole again.

We will discover a meaningful role for humans on planet Earth, when we return to claim our place in the community.

Over the past 10 years I have started to live more quietly in the countryside of Chiang Dao, Northern Thailand. I built a house that took a leaf from the air regulation of our local termite mound, so it's a cool, energy-efficient passive home. It has folding doors that open wide to give a full view of the sacred mountain of Doi Chiang Dao, which is also reflected in a pond. This is a place where I come to revive my body and soul. Then we started to revive the living soil, producing organic food alongside rewilding the wetland biodiversity, which also serves to treat the water quality flowing into our land. I combined the nicknames of both my parents to call the place "Nunienoi".

Within two years, local wild Siamese fighting fish that have not been seen in the area for some twenty years made a comeback. They were found at the end of our wetland system where the water is the cleanest after flowing through a whole series of reconstructed ponds and wet meadows. The impact of herbicides used in the area, however, is still felt at the beginning of the wetland system. Contaminated water still inhibits aquatic plant growth in the first two ponds.

Nonetheless, we have plenty of dense grassy water edge, where many water birds could lay their eggs, so their numbers have increased quickly in just a few years. They have begun to feel safer and increasingly comfortable with us, and have started to stay in the open, something which they did not dare to do before for fear of people hurting them.

Our water is clean, so dragonfly and damselfly whose nymphs need clean water can thrive. The water-edge vegetation also provides safe perches for them to cast their last moult, as the nymphs emerge from the water, fold out and dry their wings. They each feed on as many as 100 mosquitoes a day, so even though our house is set in the midst of wetland and paddy fields, we hardly get bitten by mosquitoes. We can lie comfortably outdoors at night on the balcony to gaze at the stars.

Strange species of spider hunt in our rose beds and nearby trees. We have so far recorded over 50 species, and are still counting. They seem to mimic everything. There are spiders that look like tree buds, those that look like bees, ants, scorpions, and of course one that mimics rose beetle. There are spiders that hunt with a pendulum they fashion from drops of their own saliva. These spiders eat the animals who feed on our crops.

It is exciting to see a rich array of life recovering before our eyes within only a short time. Our small team of farm workers managed to clear their old debts within the first two years they started working here. They have stories to tell everyday about wildlife on the farm. They are observant and full of knowledge, so I get to learn a lot too.

Life renews again if we give it a chance.

More than ten years have passed since that magical day in the Salish Sea. There have been experiences that I can explain and those that

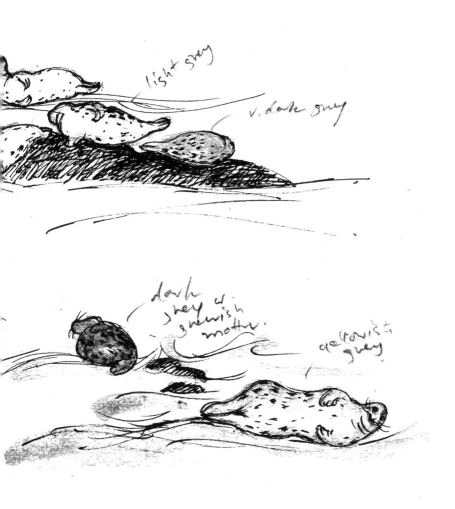

Epilogue: Towards *Homo gaia*

I cannot explain. There have been successes and failures at work in nature conservation. Through all this time, I still often think about the seal, otter, and orcas. It seems that apart from the survival routine we earthlings go about on a daily basis, there is a large planetary community bigger than the group provided by our own species, which has a shared language and a certain way of life, communicating through telepathy.

That afternoon in the Salish Sea, they tuned into a level of consciousness together and received a message of my hope. Each one of them responded in a different role: the river otter and orcas made an appearance as I had wished, while the seal took on the role of an ambassador and presenter of the show.

They came to tell me that the world where we are all connected as one is real. And that they are waiting for us to return as members of Gaia Community.

Epilogue: Towards *Homo gaia* 143

Appendix
Daily Practice Routine

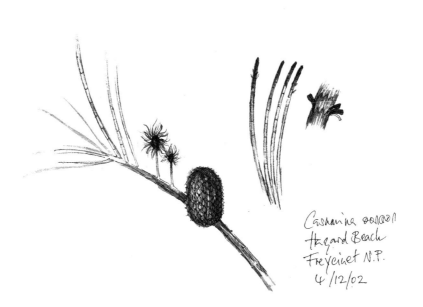

Learning to know nature takes time. It takes a continuing interest. Many nature educators tend to agree on the following two core routines, which if practice on a daily basis, will help the practitioner develop finer and sharper connections with nature. It will increase and expand your ability to receive information. The important thing is not to force yourself.

1. Sensing and observing nature at a local patch near home (sit spot)

We do not need to travel far into wilderness areas to access nature. Learning to appreciate nature nearby helps us see the magic of nature everywhere we go.

Simply find a place with nature you can readily access every day. This is to be your favourite patch to spend time with nature, which Jon Young of the Eight Shields Institute calls a 'sit spot'. To select one for yourself, consider:
- Short distance with easy access
- Safety
- A spot near a water body or feeding patch increases a chance of seeing animals

If you don't have a garden at home or do not live near a park, you can create a sit spot on an apartment balcony or even by a window sill. You can add a bird bath and flowers attractive to birds and butterflies in this spot.

Spend about half an hour here every day. Open all your senses and train them to be more acute. You could use activities given in chapter 3 to practice hearing, the feelings on skin, looking at a wide angel, at long distance, and close up to see details at different angles. Greet the life you find there, and note changes each day. Note also your feelings and emotions. Sketching to record nature observations helps.

Every week try to visit a nature spot a little further away in the local area. Get to know it. Perhaps start learning about a group of living things you're particularly interested in. It could be birds, insects, trees, or flowers. Note the changes through time.

Contemplate the things you notice and ask questions. Why is it like that? What does it remind you of? What do you need to observe more to find out the answers?

2. Reflecting on a day event (story of the day)

Review your experience with nature every day. Is there anything worth remembering? Search for "story of the day" and reflect on it. One day there may be a dramatic event, like the rare Fairy Pitta migrating through a Bangkok public park, or an exciting moment when you happen to notice a detail of a very common flower that you planted on the balcony, which you've never noticed before. Another day, nothing really happens of note. Try reflect a little. How did you feel today when sitting at the sit spot?

Reflecting and editing your observations and feelings into a narrative help giving meaning to the things you see, hear, taste, smell, and touch. They are no longer unrelated, scattered experiences. They have meanings that connect with us.

Telling stories stimulates the brain to integrate experiences we have encountered. It's a gift of *Homo sapiens*.

Share our stories with others just as our ancestors did in the evening around the fire. It creates learning together within a community. If there is no one near with whom you want to share your story, then perhaps share it on social media. You might inspire someone or might get interesting feedback to think about.

It is very different when we tell stories to others than when we keep the experience to ourselves. With others, we need to find a way to transcribe it in such a way that they can get close to receiving the same experience. It takes our own understanding of what has happened to another level. This expands further our capacity of observation in our next encounters with nature.

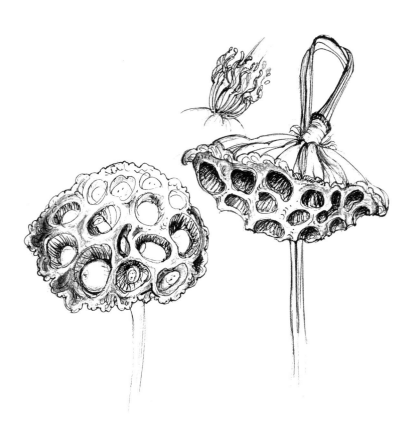

Appendix: Daily Practice Routine 147

148　Homo Gaia – REJOIN EARTH'S COMMUNITY, WHERE WE BELONG

Appendix: Daily Practice Routine

From the author

Forester Kangaroo
Maria N.P.
2/12/02

I am the last generation of city dwellers who grew up with wilderness. Seeing downtown Bangkok where I live now, it is hard to believe that right next to the house used to be a pink lotus swamp. Winters used to be cold. Strands of fog would linger on the paddy fields behind our house. During the weekends, no adults would fix our schedules. We kids would get up early and run outdoors to play all day. We had a mission to climb every tree in the area, a competition I lost to my little brother over a coconut tree. We went to the seaside for school holidays. The beach was long and wide, with a strandline full of treasures from the deep sea. In the summer, empty shells of Common Button Tops would pile up on the shore, turning the length of the entire beach pink. The tidal zone was full of sea animals to be discovered. There were sharks and dolphins swimming near the shore.

As a young teenager, we would backpack and hike up mountains. National parks then were not built up. There were just a few wooden bungalows in the middle of a huge forest. If we went to the islands, we would sleep outdoors on the beach looking up at the big, dark sky full of stars, or stay in simple bamboo huts that villagers built for hippy travellers. That was before the age of mass tourism.

I never thought these things would disappear. But they did, rapidly, in my early twenties. The change bewildered me.

I dropped my career in advertising art, and returned to school. Like many people of my generation, I got interested in ecology, which was just a tiny subject in the whole undergraduate curriculum. We became conservationists in the late 1980s.

We are the generation which Richard Louv calls "Last Child in the Woods". He was the author who got the world's attention with the concept of nature deficit syndrome. We were the last lot who grew up connected to nature, although perhaps not as deeply connected as people who grew up in the forest.

Another key factor that kept my siblings and I tied to nature, apart from the time I was born, was our mother. She instilled in us a sense of value and recognition of the rights of other species who share the world with us. She saw them as friends. In her eyes, humans were never the centre of the universe.

Throughout many decades of working for nature conservation, my colleagues and I met up with an array of challenges, from non-threatening education work to hot issues full of political conflicts on resource uses and rights abuses. We met with more failures than successes. There were small wins, but they were not enough to halt the devastation of nature. This small book is just a thin strand of hope that I pass on to the generation after me. It is the hope of the last child in the woods, that we can still recover our connection with other lives. It is not yet too late. We only need to remember. We must not forget.

The book is a result of my last five-year project on nature connection at the Green World Foundation in Thailand. Before retiring from its Chair in early 2020, my team and I had planned a whole series of training courses under the theme. Together they were to form a big picture of nature connection at different levels and dimensions. The outbreak of Covid-19, however, put the stop to the programme.

After a year had passed and the situation had not improved enough for organizing an on-site face-to-face workshop, I began thinking of writing a book instead. The title I had in mind was this one, *Homo Gaia*. It's a name that contains all I wanted to say, while keeping hope for humanity.

I sketched out the skeleton of the book in early 2021, but the first two attempts were thrown in the bin when I found I could not answer my own questions well enough. This is the merit of writing a book: it lets us know the extent of our own understanding of the topic. I got to realize in which areas I was not yet clear.

I then had to ask myself what was it going to be. Should I shelve it for the time being and wait until I had accumulated more direct experience and crystallized my understanding, or should I just write on what I know enough about now. Maybe it would open up a conversation in Thai society. If there are people interested in the same issues, we can exchange and build up further knowledge together.

This is the same situation I faced when I started my citizen science work 35 years ago, before the term was coiled. I wanted to empower young people and local communities so they could assess and take care of the local environment, and I wanted the general public to contribute in building scientific data, sharing information and insights. Many scientists in universities at the time were not comfortable with the idea. They felt the Thai public lacked the necessary understanding of field research and skills, and that the information gained would be erratic and unreliable. I totally understood their concerns, but chose to go ahead anyway. I believed that we could learn together, and it could help accelerate the development of our scientific knowledge. We would also create more able naturalists as more people get interested in the topic. In time, a new generation of specialists would develop.

It is the same with *Homo gaia* and nature connection. We don't need to understand it well before starting a public conversation. We can talk about what we know now. As we learn more and gain better insights, we can change our mind in the parts where we got it wrong.

So I drafted a new structure for the book, and tested it out in an on-line class at Silpakorn University with my ecologist colleague Dr. Kampanart Tarapoom. It received enthusiastic responses and fruitful discussions arose, even though we talked through computer screens. I would like to give a special thanks here to Dr. Kampanart and his students. Please know that you have helped with the making of this book. It was from there that I developed the idea further and sat down to write.

I have lowered my ambition with this draft. I don't try to answer questions that are too difficult. Neither do I seek to explain "super natural" phenomenon with quantum physics, which is far too complex and abstract beyond my grasp, and possibly beyond that of many readers too. I don't want to rope in sophisticated science that sounds beautiful, but is not readily comprehensible, to alienate readers, nor to use it as a scientific version of talisman to protect me from ridicule that might flood in when we talk about the "super natural".

I lowered my expectation, and stayed with the parts of my personal direct experience that I feel comfortable enough to share.

It is my hope that readers with similar experiences will come forward and tell their stories too. Personal experiences, when kept to ourselves, can easily be brushed aside as insignificant isolated incidents. They are, however, information. When pooled together, we begin to see certain common patterns. In time, they become collective knowledge.

I therefore need to thank the participants of various workshops organized by the Green World Foundation, both long and short courses. Every experience you share is valuable. Every reflection, every story, all helped me to piece together a bigger picture. Your experiences are a significant part of this book.

Thanks to Warisara Meepasanee, the principal facilitator of our course on Nature Communication. She has made inter-species communication a tangible art, partly by using her previous experience of teaching deep listening among humans to learn to listen to other beings. It makes the training grounded and practical.

Thanks for the support of my husband Vanchai Tantivitayapitak, who has given me the courage to write.

The book was first written in Thai, where a number of people provided immensely useful comments: my husband Vanchai, of course, but also friends whose opinions I highly regard, namely Adisorn Juntrasook, Sarawut Hengsawad, Tomorn Sookprecha, Niramol Moonchinda. Totally indispensable was Patchara Soongden, my Thai-language editor, who understood well that the book has to be read with the heart, and so nudged me to dig up more personal stories than I had initially cared to share, to illustrate various points in the book.

For this English edition, I am most grateful to my editor, Narisa Chakrabongse, for her patience with my terrible English grammar, her useful comments from years of experience, and her support in the publishing of the book. Big thank are also due to Belinda Stewart-Cox, my long-time friend and colleague in nature conservation, for the wonderful foreword with such a personal touch.

I also thank Gaia the Mother Earth, every animal, every tree and other plants, for continuing to try to communicate with me, no matter how often and how long I ignored their invitations. Thank you harbour seal, orca, and river otter for your appearances in response to my request that day, more than ten years ago. Thank you Job's Grove for your friendship. Thank you all of earth's living beings for never abandoning me.

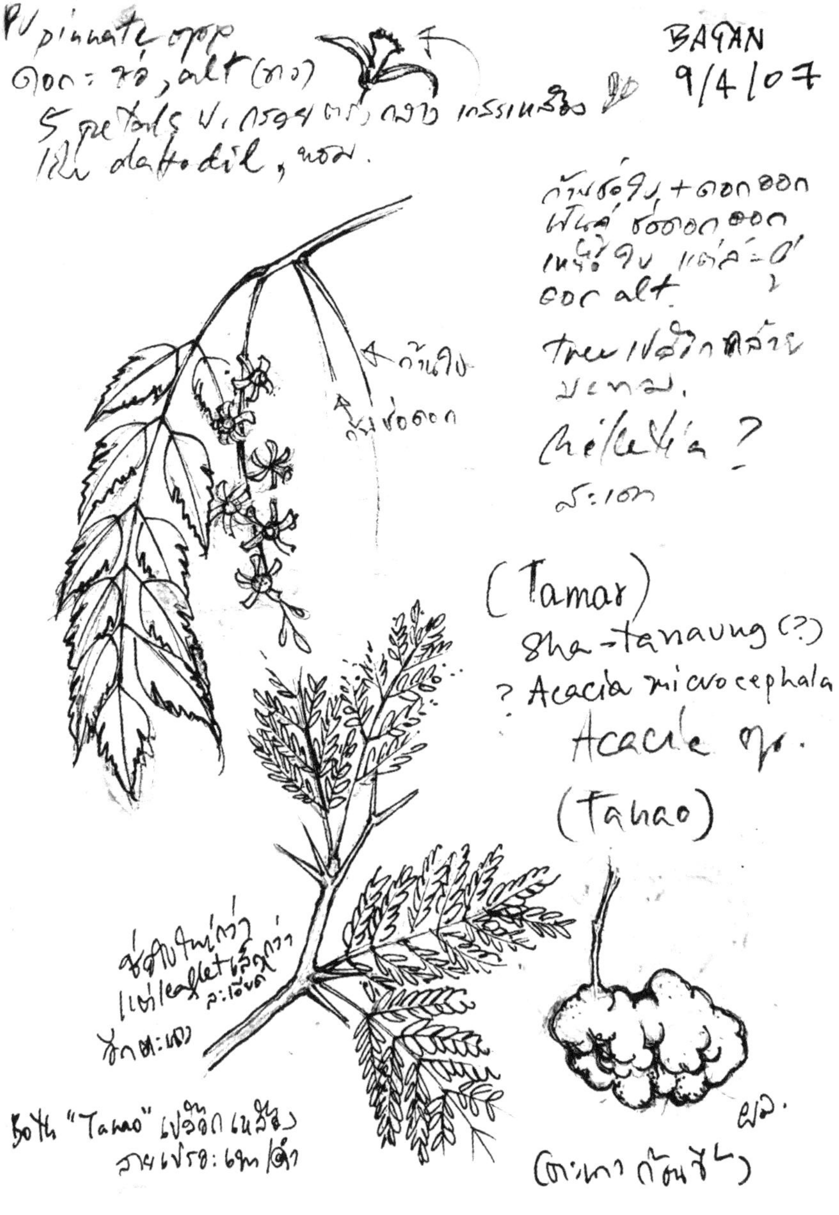
BAGAN
9/4/07
(Tamar)
Sha-tanaung (?)
? Acacia microcephala
Acacia sp.
(Tanao)